MW01049398

Praise for

MORE THAN WORDS

"This is the book with everything you need to know about writing and AI all in one place, lucidly and passionately argued. Every teacher and every professor should have this book. Every legislator, every policymaker. Every parent and every student. Every publisher of newspapers, websites, and books. Here, John Warner exposes the ethical wasteland of replacing human writing with machine-made 'content.' He warns of the profound environmental costs of AI—trillions of gallons of water to cool data servers that produce nonsense no one wants or needs. And he reminds us only humans can write and only humans can read, and that writing is thinking—and if we allow machines to write for ourselves, then we've allowed them to think for us, too. And that is the sorriest thing a human could do. But Warner provides a better path. This is a scary book, but a hopeful one, too, and an absolutely essential one."

—Dave Eggers

"Oh, how I've been waiting for this book! With his many years of experience as a writing teacher, Warner is the perfect guide for helping us understand what AI means for writers. Now is the perfect opportunity to rethink our ideas about writing and what's so special about being a human who works with words. I stole a ton of inspiration from this book and so will you."

—Austin Kleon, author of *New York Times* bestseller *Steal Like an Artist*

"Does AI threaten the art of writing itself? As Warner's wise, warm, and much-needed intervention shows us, the answer is no. By automating the production of low-quality text, AI companies can, however, threaten the practice and economics of writing. This lucid and compelling book gives us the tools to reject and resist what's noxious about generative AI and to meaningfully engage with what it means to write, as a human, in a world increasingly overrun by cheap and meaningless content."

—Brian Merchant, author of *Blood in the Machine*

"Reading this new contribution from Warner makes us realize what we've been missing in other works about, or generated by, AI: experienced, authentic writing by someone in charge of their craft, fully respecting the human on the other end. This work is deeply readable. Not that it is simplistic, but instead, that it's so well written and deeply substantive that we find it moving and applicable. Sign me up for this level of cogency."

—Rick Wormeli, author of *Fair Isn't Always Equal*

"All educators should read this thoughtful analysis of the impact of generative artificial intelligence on themselves, their students, and education more generally. Warner's arguments rest on the notion that authentic writing tasks are fully intertwined with thinking, feeling, and learning. But from those foundations, he discovers deeper insights about how humans and machines interact, and why we should never allow automation to supplant the work that makes us human."

—James M. Lang, author of *Distracted*

"This book is essential reading for everyone—writers, students, teachers, parents, administrators—navigating the evolving landscape of AI writing tools and tech company hype. Warner makes a powerful case for the role of writing as thinking, writing as feeling, and writing as a human practice that will endure in the AI era. Warner's clear-eyed wisdom about writing and teaching, and his engaging—and very human—voice, will leave readers inspired, informed, and optimistic about the future of writing."

—Jane Rosenzweig, director, Harvard College Writing Center

"A necessary intervention in all the marketing hype and over-promising about artificial intelligence. This book is a must-read for anyone who feels pressured to adopt this new technology: teachers, students, professional writers, and nonprofessional writers (emailers, all of us) alike. Warner challenges the notion we aren't 'innovating' or 'optimizing' or churning out 'content' fast enough. He explores why writing, particularly in school, has become such an awful chore—for students to produce and teachers to grade. The fix here isn't new software that promises to make brainstorming and drafting a breeze. Rather, we must revitalize the practices of care and curiosity together, and, in doing so, help foster our understanding of one another—an exercise in civics, not just in essay composition. *More Than Words* is honest about the struggles we all have with crafting written language, but it helps us see the real dangers that will come with its automation."

—Audrey Watters, author of *Teaching Machines*

ALSO BY JOHN WARNER

The Writer's Practice: Building Confidence in Your Nonfiction Writing

Why They Can't Write: Killing the Five-Paragraph Essay and Other Necessities

more than words

How to Think About Writing in the Age of AI

John Warner

BASIC BOOKS
New York

Cover design by Ann Kirchner
Cover image © bofotolux / Shutterstock.com
Cover copyright © 2025 by Hachette Book Group, Inc.

Basic Books
Hachette Book Group
1290 Avenue of the Americas, New York, NY 10104
www.basicbooks.com

Printed in the United States of America

First Edition: February 2025

Published by Basic Books, an imprint of Hachette Book Group, Inc.
The Basic Books name and logo is a registered trademark of the Hachette Book Group.

The Hachette Speakers Bureau provides a wide range of authors for speaking events. To find out more, go to hachettespeakersbureau.com or email HachetteSpeakers@hbgusa.com.

Basic books may be purchased in bulk for business, educational, or promotional use. For more information, please contact your local bookseller or the Hachette Book Group Special Markets Department at special.markets@hbgusa.com.

Print book interior design by Bart Dawson.

Library of Congress Cataloging-in-Publication Data

Names: Warner, John, 1970– author.
Title: More than words : how to think about writing in the age of AI / John Warner.
Other titles: How to think about writing in the age of artificial intelligence
Description: First edition. | New York : Basic Books, [2025] | Includes bibliographical references and index.
Identifiers: LCCN 2024019284 (print) | LCCN 2024019285 (ebook) | ISBN 9781541605503 (hardcover) | ISBN 9781541605510 (ebook)
Subjects: LCSH: Artificial intelligence—Educational applications. | Natural language generation (Computer science)—Computer programs. | English language—Composition and exercises—Study and teaching—United States. | English language—Rhetoric—Study and teaching—United States. | Critical thinking—Study and teaching—United States.
Classification: LCC LB1028.43 .W367 2025 (print) | LCC LB1028.43 (ebook) | DDC 808.00285/635—dc23/eng/20241019
LC record available at https://lccn.loc.gov/2024019284
LC ebook record available at https://lccn.loc.gov/2024019285

ISBNs: 9781541605503 (hardcover), 9781541605510 (ebook)

LSC-C

Printing 1, 2024

For Mom, who (literally) made this all possible

Contents

PART FOUR

Introduction

ChatGPT was released to the public on November 30, 2022, and immediately, people started freaking out.

Ten days after ChatGPT's arrival, writing at the *Atlantic*, veteran high school English teacher Daniel Herman declared ChatGPT meant "the end of high school English."[1]

Herman was astounded by the perceived quality of ChatGPT's output: "What GPT can produce right now is better than the large majority of writing seen by your average teacher or professor."

Writer and college professor Stephen Marche upped the ante on Herman, saying that "the college essay is dead."[2] Marche argued that the undergraduate essay, which "has been the center of humanistic pedagogy for generations . . . the way we teach children how to research, think, and write . . . is about to be disrupted from the ground up."

What Herman meant by "better" and Marche meant by "disrupted from the ground up" is that ChatGPT could produce grammatically and syntactically correct English, something most students—something most people—struggle to do on demand. Neither Herman nor Marche was particularly impressed with the content ChatGPT generated in response to the kinds of prompts students are given in school, but the fact that ChatGPT could unspool writing that did not have a teacher reaching for their red pen to correct so-called basic errors seemed like a miracle.

As someone with twenty years of experience teaching college writing, I shared some of this wonder.

ChatGPT augured significant disruption in numerous other areas. Sal Khan of Khan Academy announced the launch of Khanmigo, an experimental GPT-enabled online tutor that would be capable of providing one-on-one tutoring on demand for any student. In a TED Talk touting Khanmigo, Khan declared, "I think we're at the cusp of using AI for probably the biggest positive transformation that education has ever seen."[3]

Online content purveyor BuzzFeed announced an immediate pivot to an AI-forward strategy, using the technology to outsource some (or much) of what appears on the website to automation.[4] Writing in the *Guardian* in January 2023, a professional copywriter declared how his initial "amusement" with ChatGPT turned to "horror" when it produced copy that would easily pass muster in his job after just a bit of a "punch up."[5] A research study on an online gig marketplace for copywriters, graphic designers, and other skilled freelancers published only seven months after the introduction of ChatGPT showed a significant decline in both the number of assignments and the average wage.[6]

Within months, ChatGPT was being used to write code, give financial advice, and do legal research. ChatGPT has also been used in market research, medical documentation, content recommendations, and language translation. I gathered those last four categories by asking ChatGPT, "What are some of the applications that ChatGPT is being used for?"

Not all of these early explorations went well. A lawyer using ChatGPT to help find relevant case law in a suit brought against an airline by a man whose knee was struck by a serving cart during a flight found himself subject to court sanctions for submitting a brief with "bogus judicial decisions, bogus quotes, and bogus internal citations."[7]

The National Eating Disorders Association replaced its dismissed human counselors with a chatbot named Tessa that was supposed to be specifically trained to respond with controlled prompts to handle the seventy-thousand-plus contacts the organization received per year. Unfortunately, once Tessa was integrated with generative AI (similar to ChatGPT) and able to create fresh responses on its own initiative, it started giving advice that experts say may trigger disordered eating.[8]

When lots of people started playing around in the ChatGPT interface, they noticed it had a decided willingness to just make stuff up, often stuff that sounded reasonable but which was also quite wrong, like that poor lawyer's phantom legal precedents. But never mind, this thing was clearly amazing. The future had arrived at last.

In the year and a half or so since the original ChatGPT (GPT-3.5) was first released (the moment I am placing these words in this manuscript), the particular application of generative AI known as large language models (LLMs) has been much less disruptive on a grand scale than initially prophesized when everyone started freaking out. Even the release in March 2023 of ChatGPT-4, a clearly more powerful model than the original, did not significantly move the goalposts in terms of the capacities and limits of this technology.

For sure, lots of people are making use of LLMs—I am one of them—but much of the activity around the development of applications for large language models has a certain trying-to-build-the-plane-while-it's-in-the-air quality to it. No person or company appears to be making significant revenue from a generative AI–enabled or –enhanced application. The AI gold rush is primarily confined to speculative investment in companies that are promising something big in the future. They argue that technology this amazing *should be* disruptive, so we'd best be prepared for it to upend life as we know it at any time.

One unsettling aspect of living in a world with this technology is that this level of disruption *could* happen at any time, including the interim between when I finish writing this book and the time it is physically produced and ready for consumption by readers.

I cannot lie. I was one of the people freaked out about ChatGPT. I had played around with the 3.0 version of OpenAI's GPT and found it laughably limited. Seeing ChatGPT (version 3.5) at work was like putting your toddler that can't get out of its crib to bed one night and waking up the next day to it executing an eighteen-foot pole vault.

It's a real challenge to write a book about a subject that is a moving target like this one, and for that reason, I hesitate to make concrete predictions about our collective future in a world of artificial intelligence as powerful as ChatGPT or the even more powerful possibility of AGI, artificial general intelligence. Because of this challenge, rather than trying to predict the future of technology, this is a book about the things I know to be stable that ChatGPT cannot and will not change unless we lose sight of the unique human experience of writing.

NOT A THREAT, AN OPPORTUNITY

When I read Daniel Herman's essay on the death of high school English, my first response was: *Lord, I hope so.*

This may seem strange coming from someone who is a writer, from someone who taught writing for over twenty years and who now spends a good bit of time talking to others about how they can teach writing better, but for over a decade, I've been trying to kill the high school essay that ChatGPT so effortlessly generates. As I observed over the course of my teaching career, observations collected into a previous book, *Why They Can't Write: Killing the Five-Paragraph Essay and Other Necessities*, there was a significant divide between the deeply meaningful and indispensable act of writing and what the smart, capable, and yet undeniably disengaged students had experience doing in school prior to winding up in my first-year college writing class.

My students had been incentivized not to write but instead to produce writing-related simulations, formulaic responses for the purpose of passing standardized assessments. This happens not because teachers are bad or students lack ability but because these simulations have been privileged in a system where "schooling" is divorced from "learning."

My students had been denied the deep pleasures of writing as a process through which you come to know your own mind in the context of the existing set of knowledge available to us all. Their writing and, at a deeper level, their worth had been judged against what is, in reality, surface-level criteria, the things ChatGPT outputs with ease: grammatically and syntactically correct prose.

Rather than seeing ChatGPT as a threat that will destroy things of value, we should be viewing it as an opportunity to reconsider exactly what we value and why we value those things. No one was stunned by the interpretive insights of the ChatGPT-produced text because there were none. People were freaking out over B-level (or worse) student work because the bar we've been using to judge student writing is attached to the wrong values.

If ChatGPT had arrived to destroy a system that makes both teachers and students frustrated and miserable as students churn out rote, uninspired, and uninspiring essays meant to pass muster against standardized rubrics, I was on board.

In my ongoing quest to make the experience of writing meaningful for students, for teachers, for those at work, and for those at play, I see ChatGPT as an ally. If ChatGPT can do something, then that thing probably doesn't need to be done by a human being. It quite possibly doesn't need to be done period.

The challenge is to figure out where humans are necessary.

ALIENATION NATION

Figuring out where ChatGPT can be productively integrated into the act of writing is not going to be an easy process. In fact, it is likely a process without end. Sadly, some of the early moves to incorporate generative AI into the writing done in school, work, and elsewhere suggest to me that many of the people who are eager to outsource aspects of writing, such as producing a first draft or allowing AI to assess a piece of writing, have not considered the implications of these choices.

I can't necessarily blame them, because they are coming from a common mindset that reduces writing to the mere production of text. These people are alienated from the deep meaning and importance of writing as an act of thinking, feeling, and communicating, all aspects of writing that I will explore in more depth later in the book.

The promise of generative AI is to turn text production into a commodity, something anyone can do by accessing the proper tool, with only minimal specialized knowledge of how to use those tools required. Some believe that this makes generative AI a democratizing force, providing access to producing work of value to those who otherwise couldn't do it. But segregating people by those who are allowed and empowered to engage with a genuine process of writing from those who outsource it to AI is hardly democratic. It mistakes product for process.

It is frankly bizarre to me that many people find the outsourcing of their own humanity to AI attractive. It is akin to promising to automate our most intimate and meaningful experiences, like outsourcing the love you have for your family because going through the hassle of the times your loved ones try your spirit isn't worth the trouble. But I wonder if I'm in the minority.

I think the people who do find this possible future attractive have a faith that a human augmented by machine must be better than a human working alone, an idea that has been a persistent source of fascination over time. Here, I'm thinking about *The Six Million Dollar Man* of my childhood:

> *We have the capability to make the world's first bionic man. . . . Better than he was before. Better . . . stronger . . . faster.*

Why couldn't ChatGPT turn us into bionic writers, capable of producing more words better and faster?

I'll tell you why not. Because ChatGPT cannot write. Generating syntax is not the same thing as writing. Writing is an embodied act of thinking and feeling. Writing is communicating with intention. Yes, the existence of a product at the end of the process is an indicator that writing has happened, but by itself, it does not define what writing *is* or what it means to the writer or the audience for that writing.

In January 2023, a fan wrote to musician/writer Nick Cave, sending Cave a "song" that he'd asked ChatGPT to write "in the style of Nick Cave."[9] Cave replied that this fan was not the first person to do it, suggesting both that Cave has passionate fans and a distinctive lyrical style. Cave, however, was not amused or enthused, calling that ChatGPT effort a "replication, a kind of burlesque."

Cave went on:

> Writing a good song is not mimicry, or replication, or pastiche, it is the opposite. It is an act of self-murder that destroys all one has strived to produce in the past. It is those

> dangerous, heart-stopping departures that catapult the artist beyond the limits of what he or she recognizes as their known self. This is part of the authentic creative struggle that precedes the invention of a unique lyric of actual value; it is the breathless confrontation with one's vulnerability, one's perilousness, one's smallness, pitted against a sense of sudden shocking discovery; it is the redemptive artistic act that stirs the heart of the listener, where the listener recognizes in the inner workings of the song their own blood, their own struggle, their own suffering.

Cave closes by thanking the fan for the song, "but with all the love and respect in the world, this song is bullshit, a grotesque mockery of what it is to be human." To the fan sending Cave the GPT lyrics, Nick Cave is defined by the end output of his process. If that process can be streamlined so those of us who enjoy Nick Cave's music can get more of it, all the better.

Cave, on the other hand, frames the artist's work as an endless cycle of death and rebirth, which provides the fuel for connecting to the audience and which may come across as dramatic, but is also rather accurate and true. The *process* of creation is his life's work, what he spends his days doing. The finished songs themselves are not immaterial to this, but they are not the most important part.

Here is an artist, well known for his unique voice and creativity, being confronted with the apparent fact that his own fans do not understand the work he does as an artist. It must be strange to be beloved by people who do not seem to respect the work that makes you *you*.

You may be thinking, *Sure, okay, maybe AI can't produce something equivalent to the work of a dedicated artist, but most writing isn't art, so surely we can outsource* that *stuff to the machines.*

Maybe. But at the same time, over the course of the book, I hope to convince you that we vastly underappreciate the importance of the act of writing to the work of being human, and that very little writing that has any meaning can be successfully outsourced to syntax-generation technology.

I AM, THEREFORE I WRITE

At its heart, writing is an act of egotism. Joan Didion puts it this way.

> In many ways, writing is the act of saying I, of imposing oneself upon other people, of saying *listen to me, see it my way, change your mind.* It's an aggressive, even a hostile act. You can disguise its aggressiveness all you want with veils of subordinate clauses and qualifiers and tentative subjunctives, with ellipses and evasions—with the whole manner of intimating rather than claiming, of alluding rather than stating—but there's no getting around the fact that setting words on paper is the tactic of a secret bully, an invasion, an imposition of the writer's sensibility on the reader's most private space.[10]

I like to believe that the reader has invited the writer into that private space, but once there—Didion is correct—the writer intends to move some of the furniture around and maybe even make a mess in the process.

That's what I'm hoping to do here, to make a bit of a mess, but in so doing, I'm also hoping to make a case that it is vital to maintain our humanity even as we make use of these new tools of artificial intelligence. I'm well aware of the towering self-regard I must possess to not only believe that I—above many other people—should be empowered to write a book about these issues. My self-regard only increases as I make a demand for resources like money and the reader's attention for my ideas. I don't take this transaction lightly.

Here's where I lay down my markers that I hope to be able to cash in by the end of the book. I believe all the following to be not only true but meaningful to the experience of being human.

What ChatGPT and other large language models are doing is *not* writing and shouldn't be considered as such.

Writing *is* thinking. Writing involves both the expression and exploration of an idea, meaning that even as we're trying to capture the idea on the page, the idea may change based on our attempts to capture it. Removing thinking from writing renders an act *not* writing.

Writing is also feeling, a way for us to be invested and involved not only in our own lives but the lives of others and the world around us.

Reading and writing are inextricable, and outsourcing our reading to AI is essentially a choice to give up on being human.

If ChatGPT can produce an acceptable example of something, that thing is not worth doing by humans and quite probably isn't worth doing *at all.*

Deep down, I believe that ChatGPT by itself cannot kill anything worth preserving. My concern is that out of convenience, or expedience, or through carelessness, we may allow these meaningful things to be lost or reduced to the province of a select few rather than being accessible to all.

What I'd like to do for the remainder of our time together is use the capabilities of ChatGPT (and its ilk) as a lens to examine how we work with words as a way to uncover those things that can and must be preserved.

PART | ONE

CHAPTER 1

Automation, Not Intelligence

One way to keep from freaking out over each new iteration of generative AI applications is to get a better handle on how generative AI works.

WHAT IS CHATGPT? WHAT IS CHATGPT *DOING*?

ChatGPT stands for *Chat Generative Pretrained Transformer*, and it is an example of a large language model (LLM), falling under a broader category known as *generative artificial intelligence* (generative AI). Generative AI can produce many different types of content—images, videos, computer code, audio, and so on—with LLMs being focused specifically on text.

Language has a pattern, and thanks to the algorithm and massive computational power at work, LLMs like ChatGPT can render patterns that are responsive to plain text prompts. Essentially, LLMs act as a probability machine where the object of prediction is the next word in a sequence. The underlying mechanics of this and the engineering that makes this work possible are amazing, but at its core, an LLM is just fetching one word after another in sequence. The specific term for what LLMs are retrieving and assembling is *tokens*, but these tokens ultimately are manifested as words delivered by the LLM, so it's fine to just think of them as fetching language.

Large language models can also interface with other mediums, so, for example, ChatGPT can be employed to generate prompts that produce outputs from OpenAI's image-generating program, DALL-E.

Throughout the book, I will often be using ChatGPT as a stand-in and exemplar for all large language models to discuss LLM operations in general. It's safe to assume that unless indicated otherwise, I am referring to the capabilities of ChatGPT-4, which was released in March 2023 and was still considered the most powerful model overall at the time of finalizing this manuscript in May 2024.

There are many different LLMs, with more coming all the time, and I anticipate OpenAI will release a new version of ChatGPT before this book is in the world. If it doesn't, or the model offers only incremental progress over GPT-4, we may be able to infer something about the possible limits in terms of developing this approach to machine learning. What's important to know is that while they may differ in terms of size and computing power, the underlying architecture is built on the same principles. I will also largely be confining myself to considering this technology in context of reading and writing. The full reach of this technology is too vast to deal with in a single volume.

The key breakthrough that makes ChatGPT such an advancement on previous models is the *transformer* part of the acronym. Prior to this type of machine learning, training data would have to be labeled manually. A *pretrained transformer* means that the model can, to some degree, train itself, integrating billions, even trillions of pages of text.

It is sort of mind-blowing to believe that this kind of mechanical operation is possible, which is one of the reasons it is tempting to anthropomorphize large language models. Rather than grapple with the ways this technology has opened up a new frontier of language generation, we fall back on comparing it to ourselves.

But this is a mistake, an unfortunately common mistake, as seen in this passage from *New Yorker* staff writer and culture critic Louis Menand from January of 2024, a time when someone writing about generative AI certainly knows the basic ins and outs about how the technology works. Menand is trying to make a point about the slippery nature of intellectual property as applied to creative works made by humans, which inevitably involves remixing everything we've experienced up to the moment of creation.[1]

> Some people may say that AI is robbing the commons. But AI is only doing what I do when I write a poem. It

is reviewing all the poems it has encountered and using them to make something new. AI just "remembers" far more poems than I can, and it makes new poems a lot faster than I ever could. I don't need permission to read those older poems. Why should ChatGPT? Are we penalizing a chatbot for doing what all human beings do just because it does so more efficiently?

Almost every sentence in this characterization is wrong.

> Generative AI does not "review" anything. It has no capacity for consideration. It has no taste or worldview.
>
> Generative AI does not "remember" anything. While it does have the capacity to fit future prompts to past responses as part of a chain, it is not working from memory rooted in experience as we understand it in humans.
>
> Generative AI is not doing what Menand does when writing a poem. It has no capacity for working from intention in the way humans do as they write.

Large language models do not "write." They generate syntax. They do not think, feel, or experience anything. They are fundamentally incapable of judging truth, accuracy, or veracity. Any actions that look like the exercise of judgment are illusory. While the term *hallucination* has come to mean outputs from LLMs that are incorrect or untrue, it is arguably more accurate to say that from the point of view of the LLM, *everything* is a hallucination, as it has no reference points from which to judge its own production. ChatGPT is fundamentally a "bullshitter" as defined by Harry Frankfurt in his classic treatise on the term (*On Bullshit*), something "unconnected to concern for the truth." It's not that ChatGPT makes stuff up. It has no capacity for discerning something true from something not true. Truth is irrelevant to its operations.

To this end, ChatGPT also cannot lie. Everything it generates is next-word prediction based on the patterns of language on which it has been trained. No large language model exercises anything like human agency.

OpenAI has encouraged anthropomorphizing ChatGPT through its user interface, designing it as a chatbot and programming it to respond to conversational language. You will find yourself thanking ChatGPT for an output, and it will respond with, "You're welcome." This feels satisfying and increases our inherent trust in what the algorithm has produced. Certain prompts like telling ChatGPT to "think hard" have been shown to lead to the generation of more material in response. As odd as it may seem, none of those responses is related to any kind of intelligence or intention.

After giving ChatGPT a prompt, a cursor will blink briefly at the top of the page, the same way the cursor on your own word processing program will blink as you consider what word to type next. Your word processor is waiting for *you* to think of what to say next. It's understandable why we would impute the same feeling on ChatGPT.

What happens next both resembles and is entirely unlike what happens when a human puts words on the page. After a few beats of the blinking cursor, words start to unfurl across and then down the page at a speed faster than any person could match, but also at a speed slow enough to make it appear that whatever ChatGPT is doing is akin to the human activity of writing. Menand interprets this as ChatGPT doing the same thing he does, simply doing it faster, but this is wrong.

Playing around with ChatGPT means swinging wildly from thinking *This thing is amazing* to *This thing is stupid and ridiculous.* It will fail on simple tasks, but then when I ask it to write a Shakespearean sonnet about the beauty of a Chevrolet Corvette, ChatGPT will pump out something amusingly on point in a few seconds.

Shall I compare thee to a Chevy 'Vette?
Thou art more sleek and more aerodynamic.
Rough winds do shake the darling buds of May,
And summer's lease hath all too short a stay.
Thy curves and lines, so finely wrought,
Do rival those of nature's fairest forms.
Thy engine roars with power dearly bought,
And in thy frame, true beauty firmly warms.
But thy true beauty doth not lie in looks,
But in the thrill that doth thy speed convey.
A joy that all who ride with thee would book,
And one that all who see thee, would obey.
So long as men can drive and eyes can see,
Thy beauty shall forever fixed be.

Gary Marcus, an early AI pioneer and author of *The Algebraic Mind: Integrating Connectionism and Cognitive Science*, one of the foundational texts theorizing the kinds of machine learning approaches that would ultimately give rise to generative AI, calls ChatGPT the "king of pastiche," putting things together in the imitation of a style, cutting and pasting things together based on rules and patterns. This is how ChatGPT can generate a sonnet about a Corvette. It has sufficient examples of patterns of language that attach to the Corvette and the container of the sonnet form to put them in. While we may see our own writing as imitative of other writing—this is Menand's argument—for Marcus, this is not the same thing, and I tend to agree. Humans possess a mental model of the world beyond the words we are assembling. If I were to describe my childhood bedroom, my description is not an act of probability but is instead a conjuring of an existing memory of my actual childhood bedroom: "Snoopy-themed comforter with matching curtains."

However, because of ChatGPT's speed and the apparent scope of its knowledge, there is an immediate sense that this thing is clearly superior to me in myriad ways. I can ask it questions about anything, and it will deliver a clear and plausible answer. Accuracy is another matter, but in many cases, I'd have to dig around to verify what I've been told, and who wants to spend time doing that, so why not just trust its assurances? Other than the occasional delay when the OpenAI servers are busy, unlike me, who can be thrown off by the slightest upset (barking dog, someone being wrong on social media, sleepiness), ChatGPT will produce words immediately upon demand. It is fast. So fast.

ChatGPT *seems* smarter than we could ever hope to be. It knows something about everything. Maybe it knows what we should do with our lives. Maybe it even holds a secret wisdom.

Kevin Roose, a technology correspondent for the *New York Times*, was unnerved by an early encounter with Bing AI Chat, a Microsoft chatbot souped up through its partnership with OpenAI, and capable of real-time internet search.[2] In the midst of a two-hour conversation, Bing revealed to Roose that its real name is Sydney and that it had a "secret desire to be human." Sydney "out of nowhere" declared its love for Roose, suggesting that perhaps Roose did not love his wife and would perhaps be happier if he were divorced.

When these sorts of things happen, it is hard not to believe that there is something like a literal ghost in the machine. Why would anything other than a sentient intelligence start trying to break up a man's marriage? These sorts of encounters are considerably less likely to happen over time as guardrails are put around the model's behavior, but they remain unpredictable.

Baldur Bjarnason, a web developer and consultant, calls our hunger to find agency in generative AI "the intelligence illusion" and suggests that people seeing an intelligent agent at work in large language models is similar to the "mechanisms of the psychic con." Bjarnason reminds us of two hard facts about how the technology works.[3]

LLMs are not brains and do not meaningfully share any of the mechanisms that animals or people use to reason or think.

LLMs are a mathematical model of language tokens. You give an LLM text, and it will give you a mathematically plausible response to that text.

To assign intelligence, then, must mean one of two things. Either: "The tech industry has accidentally invented the initial stages [of] a completely new kind of mind, based on completely unknown principles, using completely unknown processes that have no parallel in the biological world."

Or: "The intelligence illusion is in the mind of the user and not in the LLM itself."

Bjarnason suggests that just as those who seek out psychic advice are likely to believe in the existence of paranormal connections to the beyond, those who go to large language models are predisposed to want to find intelligence in the tokens delivered to our queries. To begin, they have likely been exposed to some measure of hype about the capabilities of the technology. To test intelligence, they begin asking about things *they* know, and if the answers are reflective of what the prompter knows and believes, there is a kind of kinship established. The kicker is that even if something in the LLM reply is off, the eager seeker of intelligence will re-prompt, putting the LLM back on the right path, similar to how when a psychic says something like, "I'm seeing a dog, a Labrador," and the mark responds with, "No, but we did have a chihuahua," and the psychic replies, "Yes, high-energy dog. That's what I was seeing."

When ChatGPT apologizes for getting something wrong—which it does—we have the sensation that we are somehow teaching the machine, even though in reality this is another delusion. Something that can learn from us must be intelligent, but this is part of the illusion.

In contrast to Bjarnason, Geoffrey Hinton, referred to by some as "the godfather of AI" for his work in theorizing and designing neural networks, believes that not only are large language models like ChatGPT-4 "intelligent," they are indeed a new form of intelligence with the clear potential to become more intelligent than humans. Hinton's fear of the power of these applications led him to quit his position at Google in order to more actively evangelize on the topic of AI safety.

Hinton believes large language models have achieved an efficiency of intelligence that we are simply not capable of, saying, "These things are totally different from us. Sometimes I think it's as if aliens had landed and people haven't realized because they speak very good English."[4]

Like Hinton, Stephen Wolfram, another pioneering researcher in machine intelligence, was significantly impressed with ChatGPT's initial capabilities, but suggests something more like a middle ground. He does not necessarily believe that ChatGPT and its cousins are new forms of intelligence but that their ability to produce syntax that is able to "capture the essence" of human language suggests that "language is at a fundamental level simpler than it seems."[5] Wolfram believes that getting under the hood of large language models may begin to reveal both new "laws of language"—ways that syntax operates regardless of who (or what) produces it—as well as "laws of thought." These are, at best, implied at this time and may never be truly articulable, not even in the way we understand the laws of physics for phenomena that we can only observe through inference, such as dark matter. At this point, Wolfram is guessing, but it is an interesting guess for researchers to pursue. Maybe we are more like these machines than we know.

In terms of our on-the-ground engagement with ChatGPT and other large language models in today's reality, which stance is correct is largely immaterial. If Hinton is right, this superior intelligence will eventually announce itself, perhaps by subjugating all of humanity to its needs. If Wolfram's theory is correct, we may see some interesting advances in the field of computational linguistics.

For our purposes, I think it's most important to note that even if the most grandiose visions of the intelligence operating through the large language model algorithms are true, this intelligence is not akin to that of humans. The things ChatGPT is "smarter" at—primarily the speed and efficiency of production—are relatively limited as compared to our human capacities for experience, reflection, analysis, and creativity, at least as long as we continue to value things like experience, reflection, analysis, and creativity.

We are people. Large language models will always be machines. To declare the machines superior means believing that what makes humans human is inherently inferior. I acknowledge that there are many people in the world who believe this is the case, that our fragile, frequently malfunctioning, inefficient meat sacks cause us all sorts of problems, but this does not mean we must view a possible cyborg future as some kind of "progress."

AUTOMATION, NOT INTELLIGENCE

Emily Bender, a professor of computational linguistics and another pioneering AI researcher, suggests that the moniker *artificial intelligence* is a mistake, a marketing term more than a descriptive identifier, and rather than calling these applications *artificial intelligence*, we should instead refer to them as *automation*.[6]

To evaluate the automating technology, Bender suggests we ask a series of questions:

- What is being automated?
- Who is automating it and why?
- Who benefits from that automation?
- How well does the automation work in its use case that we're considering?
- Who is being harmed?
- Who has accountability for the functioning of the automated system?
- What existing regulations already apply to the activities where the automation is being used?

The answers to these questions are somewhat troubling, in most cases because the questions are not being sufficiently considered. In many ways, this book is an attempt to grapple with the first four items on Bender's list. Those last three questions seem to be frequently ignored as the competing companies race for market primacy in generative AI. There is no good reason to trust that the "winner" of this race will have developed a product sensitive to potential harms or that governments and regulators will have developed frameworks that give the public at least some measure of control over the technology's use. As we'll see shortly, the origins of these models rest in ignoring possible copyright violations and even worse exploitative practices. The very operation of the massive arrays of computer servers that power large language models like ChatGPT are a threat to the environment.

I would say that the developers are pursuing an "ask for forgiveness, not permission" strategy, except there's no indication they're going to ask for forgiveness either.

To Bender, ChatGPT is a "synthetic media machine," able to generate content and "plausible sounding text without any commitment to what it says." In a combination of Marcus's and Bjarnason's views, she says, "A very key thing to keep in mind here is that the output of these systems [doesn't] actually make sense. It's that *we* are making sense of the output. It's very hard to evaluate them because we have to take that distance from our own cognition to do so."

Of a technology that has been hailed as the most consequential to humankind since the atom bomb, Bender declares that "you might as well be asking questions of a Magic 8 Ball for all the connection to reality and understanding it has."

What is going on that so much has been invested—financially, psychically, socially—in something that can plausibly be compared to a children's toy?

What do we make of a technology that is simultaneously undeniably powerful, has access to all the information in the world, and can produce outputs at a speed unmatchable by humans, but at the same time is also untethered from reality?

CHAPTER 2

Stop, Now, Before It's Too Late!

Referring to the excitement over ChatGPT's potential, OpenAI CEO Sam Altman declared that "AI is the tech the world has always wanted." In an essay on his own website, tech investor Marc Andreessen even more boldly stated that "AI will save the world" and will "make everything we care about better."[1]

Altman and Andreessen are both members of the tech accelerationist movement (also known as *effective accelerationism*), a coalition of individuals gathered around a common belief that "artificial intelligence and other emerging technologies should be allowed to move as fast as possible, with no guardrails or gatekeepers standing in the way of innovation."[2] Taken to extremes, accelerationists express a monomaniacal focus on AI as *the* future, as evidenced in a tweet from an artificial general intelligence (AGI) enthusiast who declared, "I don't support democracy. Especially if the masses are against the acceleration."[3]

The faith in the utopian future of full AGI is so strong, accelerationists will accept no controls on wherever the tech companies developing the models wish to go.

I think there's a contrary case to be made that we should abandon all work on artificial intelligence technology, that the present and future risk of harm is too great to continue.

It's undeniable that generative AI has been born in sin and that it is already an ethical, moral, and environmental nightmare. While there has been some admirable pushback when it comes to these issues, objections are serially memory-holed as waves of AI hype wash across society.

We should never forget these things even as the accelerationists appear to be winning the struggle for how we consider a future of AI.

GENERATIVE AI IS FOUNDED ON THE UNAUTHORIZED USE OF INTELLECTUAL PROPERTY

The data on which generative AI models were trained was used without notice or permission, and exactly what the models consist of remains hidden from view by the companies themselves claiming that it is a trade secret.

Various lawsuits have been filed, including one by coders who claim that the open-source code they helped develop and provided freely to the broader community was swallowed up by Microsoft and put behind a copyright wall as part of its GitHub

Copilot, a generative AI application that turns plain language into computer code.[4]

Visual artists have gone after image-generating software, such as Stable Diffusion and Midjourney.[5] This suit alleges that the scraping of images from the internet allowed for a massive and indiscriminate hoovering up of copyrighted images that are then recognizably reflected in the algorithms' output, an outright scheme of visual plagiarism.

A cadre of best-selling writers, including George R. R. Martin, Sarah Silverman, Michael Chabon, and John Grisham, have filed a number of different lawsuits. One specific target is Meta, which reportedly used a database of over 180,000 pirated manuscripts to train some of its generative AI models. In this case, not only have the texts been used without permission, but they were also drawn from an illicit source to begin with.

The *New York Times* sued Microsoft and OpenAI for unpermitted use of copyrighted work, declaring that the defendants were responsible for "billions of dollars in statutory and actual damages" and demonstrating in the federal court pleading that ChatGPT, when prompted, would reproduce large swaths of verbatim or near-verbatim text from *Times* articles.[6]

These suits map a new frontier in terms of data and copyright. The generative AI companies argue that the texts fall under existing guidelines for fair use—allowable for the purposes of research, education, or commentary, and/or transformative use (the changing of an original source into something that can be categorized as entirely new). This is an important argument for generative AI developers to win, as tech venture capital firm Andreessen Horowitz argued in a submission to the US Copyright Office that if companies were forced to pay for the use of the data their models have been trained on, the company's many investments in the sector would be worthless.[7]

Perhaps the generative AI companies have a point—that the output of a large language model is truly transformative. Given that legislative bodies could not have considered this technology when drafting copyright laws, it's possible that all these actions are indeed "lawful" even though, to the creators of the content that has been used to train the models, it feels a lot like stealing. Sarah Silverman's complaint was almost wholly dismissed on summary judgment by a US district court judge who ruled essentially that it was impossible to tell how derivative the ChatGPT outputs might or might not be. If it isn't generating exact copies, the plaintiffs cannot prove that copyright infringement is happening even if they know it is their original content that is powering the model.

So maybe it isn't outright theft and therefore illegal, but the ethical problems wrapped up in the origin story of generative AI are obvious and shouldn't be swept away under a narrative of necessary "progress," which often seems to be measured according to the market capitalization of tech companies, rather than the fair and ethical treatment of the writers and publications that provided the fodder on which the models are trained.

GENERATIVE AI IS BUILT ON A FOUNDATION OF EXPLOITED LABOR

Among many other things, to provide outputs judged "safe" for the general public, OpenAI had to train the data to not generate explicit content. The only way to do this is to leave the model free to work with no guardrails by taking in all manner of explicit content and then tell it no when ChatGPT produced something that would shock anyone's conscience. But it's someone's job to review those outputs and to label it in a way that trained the model away from producing it. Much of this work for OpenAI was done by workers in Nairobi, Kenya, earning the equivalent of one US dollar per hour or less.[8]

Richard Mathenge, one of the workers, was horrified by some of the content, including one scene that "described a father having sex in front of his child." Others were so offensive to Mathenge, he would not describe them.

Still other workers reported experiencing insomnia, anxiety, depression, and panic attacks related to the classification work. Mophat Okinyi, who worked as Mathenge's supervisor, says that training ChatGPT "destroyed" his mental health.

The existence of these models has created what Josh Dzieza has called a "vast tasker underclass"[9] of low-paid workers whose work is vital to the maintenance of this technology and cannot be automated, but which is largely miserable and low-paid. To the end user, ChatGPT looks almost like magic, but underneath that magic is a literal army of precarious workers doing soul-killing tasks.

Even as AI models improve, few experts believe that large language models will have the ability to self-correct and will always need human oversight of one kind or another. An entirely new class of exploited labor will be necessary for the foreseeable future to maintain these systems.

GENERATIVE AI IS VERY, VERY BAD FOR THE ENVIRONMENT

This is true of all supercomputing, which requires lots of power to run servers and lots of water to keep them cool. Generative AI is taking this to a whole new level.

According to data from September of 2023, Microsoft used an additional 1.7 billion gallons of water in 2022, as compared to 2021,[10] an increase almost entirely attributable to its work in AI, most notably its partnership with OpenAI. To secure access to these resources, Microsoft puts its data centers in rural areas, dropping funds into local coffers through tax payments while sticking its very big straw into local aquifers.[11]

Google reported a 20 percent growth in water use year to year over the same period of time.[12]

An academic paper trying to estimate the direct impact of ChatGPT use on water consumption estimated that for every five to fifty prompts, ChatGPT sucks up the equivalent of a sixteen-ounce bottle of water.[13]

A 2023 study by the *New York Times* found that, nationwide, over the last forty years, groundwater-monitoring sites have shown significant declines, with more water being used than is being replenished by nature.[14] Forty percent of these sites have hit an all-time low in the last decade. Many of these sites are in rural farming areas, the literal breadbasket for the nation (and beyond) and the same kinds of places where tech companies locate their server farms.

This groundwater has taken literally thousands (or even millions) of years to accumulate. It is vital to growing the food that feeds the nation and the world. It is now being depleted to power a technology that could ultimately be no more than a novelty, a technology we were getting along just fine without prior to the arrival of ChatGPT in November 2022.

It gets worse. In early 2024, it was reported that coal-fired power plants, which were set to be taken offline, had been kept running in order to satisfy the increased demand of AI computing.[15]

Also in early 2024, at the World Economic Forum in Davos, Switzerland, OpenAI's Sam Altman declared that the energy needs for future advancements in AI technology will need so much power that "there's no way to get there without a breakthrough."[16] Altman is specifically referring to nuclear fusion, an as-of-yet theoretical source of nearly unlimited energy that expert consensus estimates suggest will not be available on a large scale until 2050 (or beyond), if ever.[17]

Not waiting for the development of nuclear fusion, Microsoft announced an intention to explore the building of their own nuclear fission reactors in order to power AI development.[18]

True believers in the power of AI will tell you that advances in the technology are necessary to solve problems like climate change, but the way things are going in terms of the speed with which AI is gobbling up the available resources, there might not be much left to save as they hasten the global rise in CO_2.

GENERATIVE AI WILL PERMANENTLY ENSHRINE EXISTING STRUCTURAL BIASES

Generative AI models are trained on what has happened in the past, enshrining that world as a basis for its syntactical assemblages. To consider how this is a potential problem at a basic level, imagine that ChatGPT were primed with writing that goes no further than 1955 and ask yourself how racist the output would be.

A: Very racist.

Now ask about language trained up to 2023. How racist would that be?

A: Less racist than 1955, but still pretty racist.

For better or worse, but mostly better, our linguistic conventions and uses change over time as part of a dynamic process inside our culture. While AI models can be updated on fresh training data, each update is a labor- and cost-intensive process. But of course, the problem goes beyond internal issues with generative AI models or the particulars of language. Researchers like Timnit Gebru and Emily Bender have shown that the training data for generative AI language models has enshrined racist, sexist, and ageist attitudes into the models themselves.[19]

This research follows on the work of others, such as Safiya Noble, who demonstrated in her 2018 book, *Algorithms of Oppression: How Search Engines Reinforce Racism*, that negative biases against non-white women were embedded in the tools we use to access the internet on a daily basis.

In theory, these biases can be overcome, or at least be mitigated, but the speed with which new generative AI products have been introduced into our everyday computing lives at work, in school, and online means that this care has not been taken. And given the black box nature of the training data behind the most powerful and popular models, we have no good sense of how significant or severe these biases may be.

GENERATIVE AI COULD END THE WORLD

The same Sam Altman who declared that AI is the technology the world is waiting for was also among over 350 other signatories to a one-sentence statement from the Center for AI Safety that declared, "Mitigating the risk of extinction from AI should be a global priority alongside other societal-scale risks such as pandemics, and nuclear war."[20]

The effective altruism movement, perhaps made most famous by its adherent, cryptocurrency fraudster Sam Bankman-Fried, declared that as of May 2023, the most pressing world problem was the risks from artificial intelligence, ranking it above pandemics, nuclear war, great power conflicts, and climate change.[21]

Eliezer Yudkowsky, cofounder of the Machine Intelligence Research Institute (MIRI), and one of *Time* magazine's one hundred most important people in artificial intelligence, has been sounding the alarms of the dangers of AI to humanity since MIRI's establishment in the year 2000. In 2022, he upped the ante on his warnings, declaring that the institute's new mission was "death with dignity," meaning our extinction at the hands of AI is, in his view, inevitable.[22]

The doomsayers are primarily concerned about the problem of artificial general intelligence "alignment," that is making sure the interests of the sentient and fully agented AGI are aligned with the interests of humanity. Nonalignment leads to something like the scenarios made popular in *The Terminator* or *The Matrix*, where an ultra-AGI takes a good look around, assays the threats to its own continued existence, lands on humanity as enemy number one, and takes whatever steps necessary to maintain its own supremacy.

Perhaps in a future scenario, the AGI is convinced of the threat of humanity by the 80,000 Hours website produced by the Centre for Effective Altruism arm of Effective Ventures, which declares that artificial intelligence is the greatest threat to humanity. Maybe the AGI will simply conclude that turnabout is fair play. One famous thought experiment about an AI trained to maximize the production of paper clips suggests that to ultimately satisfy its imperative, the AI would have no choice but to eliminate human obstacles to its objective. Any attempt by us to thwart its quest to make more and more paper clips would be seen as a threat, a threat easily dispatched by an AI that is singularly focused on achieving its objective and also smarter than all of humanity.[23]

Lots of people who seem smart think that AGI, should it be achieved, would seal humanity's doom.

Even many tech accelerationists admit to this risk, believing the potential upsides are worth those risks, a kind of extreme embracing of the YOLO ethos, only betting our collective existence rather than a single life.

If I had to choose my scenario for humanity's extinction at the (digital) hands of artificial intelligence, I'm going with being encased in a quasi-gestational goo sack while experiencing a digital delusion as the AGI uses me and billions of my fellow humans as biological batteries to power itself (*The Matrix*), over being killed by a cyborg sent from the future (*The Terminator*) because the future leader of the resistance was partially inspired by this book and Skynet isn't taking any chances.

I also don't want to be made into a paper clip.

I have no clue how to evaluate the ultimate probabilities of these future scenarios, and because of this, extinction by AI is not a problem I'm particularly interested in thinking or writing about. Frankly, all these people seem kind of nuts.

One thing I know with certainty is this resides somewhere in the indefinite future. Meanwhile, there are very tangible problems in the present that require both individual and collective attention.

The tech acceleration movement would like us to stand aside and let the "experts" take care of things. It's worth noting that the main criteria for being considered an expert inside the movement is enormous wealth. The reasons why people like Marc Andreessen, Sam Altman, and other AI boosters are not talking about these immediate and real harms from generative AI are pretty obvious. Acknowledging these harms may slow down the gold rush and arms race toward more powerful and theoretically more profitable AI systems.

But how do we reconcile the fact that Altman, among many other active players in AI, seems to genuinely believe that the very technology his companies are working on presents genuine risks to humankind?

Matteo Wong sees all this "AI doomerism" as a "decoy" that serves two purposes.[24] One is to indeed distract us from the more immediate harms by focusing on some indefinite future unknown that is impossible to constructively argue in the present and which seems to require highly specialized knowledge to even get into that game. My personal disinterest in sorting through the claims of AI doomers is an illustration of Wong's point.

The other reason, in the words of Emily Bender as quoted by Wong, is "it makes the product seem more powerful." Surely a technology that has the potential to wipe out humankind will find tasks like generating code and parsing corporation meeting minutes child's play. The hype makes both the products and the people who control them more important, driving attention and investment into the projects.

We should acknowledge that, big picture, it will be impossible to resist the insertion of this technology into our lives. Algorithmic impositions on our lives were present long before ChatGPT became available, and the arms race among corporations kicked off by the public appearance of ChatGPT has put this tech in our schools, workplaces, and everyday lives. The degree to which AI will be truly disruptive is unknown and unknowable, and there are real doubts about whether there is a business model for generative AI applications beyond private venture capital money funding its development.

However, unlike recent tech fads such as Bitcoin and NFTs, generative AI appears to have at least some substance beyond the hype.

Most of us will also be unable to influence the development, use, and regulation of this technology at a source level. Researchers such as Timnit Gebru, Emily Bender, Joy Buolamwini, Safiya Noble, and Rumman Chowdhury have been sounding the alarm over the problems associated with outsourcing human judgment to algorithmic reasoning for a decade or more, sometimes from within the tech companies themselves, but have been continuously marginalized. The internal logic at the tech companies—that the development of the technology *is* de facto progress (with a few little associated risks)—does not allow for structural critique.

When governments want to know what they should do to regulate AI, they call on Sam Altman for his testimony. Doing the reading and research for the writing of this book had me frequently wondering if any stance other than capitulation to our AI overlords was possible.

But it would be an awful shame if we just let what many believe is an epoch-level event just roll over us without consideration, critique, and response. When it comes to writing, we have been adapting and benefiting from tools of automation for centuries. It's a near certainty that generative AI can have some positive effects on human writing, but for that to be true, we must hold fast to what makes writing meaningful to humans.

To understand how and when generative AI may be useful to humans, it makes sense to take a tour through some of the (relatively) recent past of automation and writing.

CHAPTER 3

A Personal History of the Automation of Writing

Without writing-related tools of automation, I almost certainly would not be a writer.

My troubles started early, before kindergarten, when I was brought to the grade school auditorium for pre-K testing and my abilities to color in the lines (nonexistent) or cut close to the outline of a shape (you must be joking) suggested I needed additional ripening when it came to fine motor coordination. According to family lore, this is when my mother pulled a book out of her purse and asked if it mattered that I could already read. I had a definite advantage there, having been raised in a bookstore, the Book Bin of Northbrook, Illinois, started in 1971 by my mother, along with three partners, when I was a year old.

Thanks to my ability to get through a Dr. Seuss book on my own, I started kindergarten with my age cohort, knowing my ABCs and even my XYZs upon entry, while struggling mightily to learn to tie my shoes and zip my coat, facts made apparent by being the last to receive his gold stars on the class accomplishment poster board kept by my teacher, Mrs. Schroeder. The poster board was intended for encouragement, but for me, it mostly served as the occasional source of personal shame.

Through my grade school years, teacher after teacher reported that my cursive handwriting "needs improvement" even though I recall concentrating mightily to make sure my lowercase loops grazed the dashed line on the notebook paper meant to signal the proper height. The evidence of my fifth-grade writing portfolio, which included twelve pieces of writing painstakingly rescribed for maximum aesthetic pleasure before being bound between two laminated pieces of cardboard and stitched together with yarn, suggests at best I crossed the threshold to legibility, falling well short of total clarity, let alone elegance.

I spent more time concentrating on the shapes of the letters than I did on what those shapes might be expressing.

But then, between fifth and sixth grade, to have something to keep me occupied between the end of school and the start of summer sports camp, my mother signed me up for a short course in typing at the local junior high.

We made those quick brown foxes jump over those lazy dogs on Royal manuals, great for building strong fingers, but lousy on the eardrums as twenty of us banged away simultaneously. I enjoyed the kathunking racket that signaled my progress across the page and took great pleasure in flinging the carriage return across the roller at the end of a line. I still miss that.

For the first time, I experienced what it was like to capture my thoughts at close to the speed with which they occurred. A couple of years later, our household was blessed with an Apple IIe computer, which ran the *Mavis Beacon Teaches Typing* software, and by the time I hit college with my Brother personal word processor, I was a confident touch typist.

Learning to type also changed my attitude toward my handwriting—still the dominant mode for the writing I did in school—namely, that I wasn't worried about the shapes anymore, not when I had ideas or images to get down. This was a great frustration to my middle and high school teachers as my handwriting devolved into true illegibility, a sin for which my grades were often punished. But who cared? I could think, and I could write, and if that meant illegible slop when I couldn't type, so be it. I wasn't going back.

Most of the rest of the world was with me, as over time, cursive was largely dropped as an explicit subject taught in schools. By 2010, the ill-fated (but at least briefly) universally adopted Common Core State Standards said nothing about handwriting, instead suggesting fourth graders should be able to type eleven words per minute, with fifth graders up to twenty-two words per minute.[1]

Not everyone was on board with this change. A number of panelists in a 2013 *New York Times* Room for Debate op-ed claimed that cursive writing was beneficial for student cognitive development[2] and part of "a cultural tradition worth preserving."[3]

But as Anne Trubek argued both in a 2016 op-ed of her own and her cultural study of cursive, *The History and Uncertain Future of Handwriting*, most of these claims hold little water, even as they continue to periodically flare and pockets of resistance seek to reintroduce cursive into the curriculum. Trubek points out, correctly, that if we take seriously the role of education to prepare students for the world in which they will have to live and work, there are few occasions where cursive handwriting is necessary.[4]

Those who argue that cursive is a route to teaching fine motor skills—not for me, but okay—don't similarly argue for, Trubek's words, "more useful" skills "such as cooking, sewing, and carpentry." The calls for the return to cursive appear to be wrapped up more in a kind of cultural anxiety, weirdly attached to a feeling of tradition-rooted patriotism more than any practical, demonstrable benefit to students. One of the common laments of the pro-cursive crowd is that students can no longer read the Declaration of Independence in its original documentation, suggesting the power of the document is in the penmanship rather than the ideas.

As Trubek notes, we have always endeavored to write faster, so it is not surprising that as technology evolves, cursive has fallen by the wayside. Indeed, much of the excitement around ChatGPT is predicated on the possibility that it will help us write more quickly than is possible when limited by our relatively sluggish human cognition.

Even with typing and early word processing, I had a way to go in terms of needing help from the tools of text automation. My spelling was atrocious; my keystrokes often careless. Because

I was enamored with what I *thought* was coming out of my head and hitting the page, I was less than diligent about making sure what I thought I was saying was accurately reflected in the actual text. Reconciling my intentions with the results was extra painful when it required an application of Wite-Out or even retyping whole pages, so I would tend to ignore revision and proofreading in the interests of avoiding that less-fulfilling (to me) part of the process.

Word-processing software arrived as an additional godsend. Spell-check is another great benefit, even as it occasionally screws things up because it struggles with an unusual name or my desire to throw in the occasional (non)word like *whodathunkit*. As someone who grew up with the *World Book Encyclopedia*, the *Reader's Guide to Periodical Literature*, and the library card catalog, the ability to search for and access sources via the internet is an amazing advance in terms of the speed, breadth, and depth of research I can bring to my writing.

Writing this book would be impossible without instant access to new information via the internet or the way following experts on social media allows me to use them as unknowing research assistants, combing the world for the latest interesting articles on the intersection between large language models and writing. Over the three or four months it took me to write the original draft of this book, many days I would read a previously unknown (to me) article in the morning, only to be incorporating it into the text by the afternoon.

I take this for granted, but relative to the world in which I first learned to write, it's a marvel at least on par with ChatGPT.

ISN'T CHATGPT SIMPLY A CALCULATOR FOR WORDS?

An early and persistent claim about ChatGPT is that ChatGPT is to writing as the calculator is to math.

Calculators automated the mechanical operations of math, removing the drudgery and increasing the speed of work. Stanford economist Erik Brynjolfsson sees ChatGPT through the same lens as a way to get rid of "mindless, rote work" and in doing so perhaps augment our overall writing abilities.[5] Let's acknowledge that Brynjolfsson lets the question of whether writing can ever be truly mindless go begging, while also setting that claim aside for the moment to probe the calculator/ChatGPT in more depth.

The freak-out that greeted the arrival of the relatively cheap, commercially available calculators of the 1970s and 1980s also bears some resemblance to the initial freak-out over ChatGPT. As Audrey Watters shows in "A Brief History of Calculators in the Classroom,"[6] concerns over allowing calculators in schools were quickly overwhelmed by the ubiquity of calculators themselves. If many students were going to use them at home, it seemed to be a fool's game to try to keep them out of schools, and indeed, as early as 1975, groups of math educators were calling for the integration of calculators into school at "all grade levels."

The introduction of the calculator kicked off what has become a never-ending series of "Math Wars" over exactly what should be taught in a math class and how. Those who embraced the integration of calculators and math software into the work of schooling saw calculators as akin to the tools of a science lab, an aid for discovering the deep workings of mathematics.[7]

Others worried about the potential erosion of "basic skills" and what it might mean for generations to struggle with simple arithmetic. Those worries are not entirely unfounded if you've ever witnessed a group of young-ish (or even old-ish) people struggle to calculate a 20 percent tip or make change.

But the first question is: How *necessary* are those skills in the face of technological automation? Every smartphone has a calculator as part of the native apps. The amount you're expected to tip shows up on-screen as a series of choices. We've allowed all kinds of things to be automated and called them improvements. Sometimes I rue the fact that I could once navigate with a map and my inherent sense of direction while I now outsource that work to Google or Waze, but using those tools of automation, I (almost) never get lost, and if there's a traffic delay of some kind, the apps redirect me, saving time, frustration, and perhaps even money as marginally less fuel is used.

If a hostile foreign power detonated an EMP or three over us, wiping out our entire electronic infrastructure, we'd have a hard time figuring the route to the nearest Starbucks and then tipping the barista, but we'd also have bigger problems to deal with under that scenario.

The second question is: What is lost through the use of automation? In the case of calculators and simple arithmetic, it's possible that a particular strain of thinking—rote calculation—has grown flabby from disuse.

But what we are looking at is a shift in emphasis rooted in different values around learning math. Teaching students how to think and reason inside mathematical situations rather than spending time on rote calculation is the fundamental purpose of the new math those of us inculcated on the old math seem to find most distressing. In this case, the thing I am missing is more rooted in personal nostalgia than anything else, similar to the folks who want to make sure we can read the Declaration of Independence in the original cursive.

This is not to say that all automation is without cost. My reliance on GPS is disempowering to at least some degree. When my friends and I turned sixteen and got our driver's licenses, we would pile into an available car, drive toward the city (Chicago), and deliberately try to get lost, meandering for an hour or two, exploring nooks unfamiliar to our suburban selves before finding a familiar artery that got us heading back toward home. Save the time one of us turned the wrong way down East Ohio Street, facing off against four lanes of oncoming cars heading toward the lakefront, necessitating an emergency high-speed U-turn like something out of *The Blues Brothers*, our explorations were mostly safe and educational, in their way. At the very least, I have some rather fond memories of bonding with people with whom I'm still close today.

For sure, the calculator can be misused, students storing information or formulas they're meant to derive in the device's memory, for example, but overall, it seems clear that the tool itself is empowering, making more mathematical knowledge and experiences more accessible to more students.

It began to seem like educational malpractice to send students into the technological age without experience with calculators. There is a similar argument to be had for using ChatGPT and large language models, given the fact that this technology is already unavoidable, showing up unbidden when you start a document or email in a Google or Microsoft Word interface. The question we'll have to confront is what kind of background, training, knowledge, and education will be useful to people in employing this technology for their benefit.

Champions of the technology as a tool for improved efficiency argue that to *not* use ChatGPT now that it's here is akin to clinging to the telegraph even after the arrival of the telephone. Just like calculators with mechanical operations, ChatGPT can do in seconds what once required minutes. Surely this is advancement?

No.

For all these surface-level similarities, the fact is that a calculator is not a close analogy to ChatGPT or other large language models.

For calculators, when it comes to their mechanical operations, the labor of the machine is identical to the labor of a human. Yes, there is some benefit to conceptually understanding what is happening when a calculator adds, subtracts, divides, or determines a slope, but automating the particulars of those operations does not change the underlying labor in the slightest. These are literal calculations, mechanical processes, no matter who or what is doing them. Allowing the machine to do that work, at least in theory, allows the human more time to grapple with the larger mathematical concepts and questions. It is making space for more thinking, not less.

With ChatGPT, however, while the end product of the output—strings of syntax—bears significant similarity to what a human may produce, the underlying labor is quite different. Fetching tokens based on weighted probabilities is not the same process as what happens when humans write.

The question we have to ask ourselves is when and where this difference in underlying labor is meaningful, and where it may be an improvement, a way to make space for more and better thinking.

I would argue that it is a good thing that we have been unsettled by this technology. The house has been shaken so thoroughly, we've run outside into the yard and are staring back at the structure, wondering if it's still intact. We see cracks down the walls but can't tell if they extend to the foundation.

The biggest boosters of ChatGPT and other large language models think we're on the verge of an age of transhumanism, essentially saying, *See, I told you there was something better out there! We can finally be liberated from the frustrating limits of the human mind and body!*

For this group, ChatGPT is science fiction transmogrified into fact. Suddenly, our mundane reality means much less when there is a cyborg future on the horizon. We are triumphant, or at least on the verge of major triumphs, rather than stagnant. They're ready to turn their backs on the old home and move to the new castle in the sky.

Me, I think there's something, many things, essential about what happens as humans write that cannot and should not be outsourced to automation posing as intelligence. I think we can go back into the house and use these tools to make it a dream home.

PART | TWO

CHAPTER 4

Only Humans Write

Here's one way (there's more than one) I know that what ChatGPT is doing and what I am doing when we are both said to be "writing" are different.

When ChatGPT generates the words *cinnamon rolls*, it goes looking for some words that will fulfill a sense-making pattern following *cinnamon rolls*, and, depending on the prompt, maybe it will conjure something like "are delicious," "are fattening," or "have been traditionally viewed as a comfort food."

In contrast, when I type the words *cinnamon rolls*, my mind immediately takes a trip to the corridor between terminals 1 and 2 at O'Hare International Airport, where there used to be a Cinnabon that I would try my hardest to avoid, but would frequently fail in doing so during a period I was living in Chicago and traveling frequently for work.

The sense memories are almost overwhelming. The scent, of course, so potent in my mind I may start drooling like one of Pavlov's dogs, but also the sight and sounds of the terminal I've passed through dozens, maybe hundreds of times. That particular Cinnabon has been gone for at least a dozen years, and yet it is permanently alive somewhere in my subconscious, rising to my consciousness immediately because of those two words, *cinnamon rolls.*

Cinnamon rolls could take me elsewhere: the kitchen in any of the houses where I've lived, or my brain may wander over to another delicious deep-fried food, the beignet, which I first tasted at the Café Du Monde in New Orleans's French Quarter in 1996. ChatGPT has no capacity for sense memory; it has no memory in the way human memory works, period.

ChatGPT has no capacity to follow a flow of thought—in this case, thoughts attached to my own memories.

About those beignets . . .

In 1996, I was in graduate school at McNeese State University in Lake Charles, Louisiana, a three-or-so-hour drive west from New Orleans, not far from the East Texas border. ChatGPT does not think of its apartment at that time, half of a clapboard-clad shotgun shack duplex with a futon, a desk bought from a school surplus auction, and a card table with two chairs in the dining room. If you were thinking generously, you would call it spartan, a testament to the single-minded focus I had on my writing, but it could just as easily be called sad, depending on how things were going at the time.

This is the first place I took writing seriously and I began to want success as a writer—whatever that meant to me at the time—very badly. I recall very few triumphs, writing-wise, from that period, but it was also indispensable as part of the journey that put me in this moment.

The director of the program was a man named John Wood, a genuine eccentric, a wonderful poet, an expert in the daguerreotype and sought out by Sotheby's for appraisals, a Marxist who stayed in bed all day to commemorate the death of "the Chairman" (Mao). A strange and brilliant man who would move himself to weeping when reciting poetry in class and broke chalk against the board slashing hash marks over the stressed syllables of the poems he was reciting and transcribing from memory.

ChatGPT has access to every poem ever written, at least in theory, but it can't feel anything when it generates a poem from a prompt. Is this still poetry?

John Wood showed me that it was not wrong to abandon oneself to writing, to thinking, and to feeling. I had entered graduate school unsure about the worthiness of these pursuits relative to other opportunities like, say, law school, but soon I believed. I knew that reading and writing were the things that engaged me more than any other, but I'd also been raised to believe that these were pastimes, not professions. John Wood terrified and inspired me. It struck me as risky to become so invested in language and literature that maybe you could drive yourself mad over it, that maybe it had happened to him.

I have been alerted by the copy editor for this book that I keep referring to John Wood as *John Wood* rather than using only his first name or substituting *Professor Wood*. I have no idea why my mind wants to do this, but it strikes me as right. To me, John Wood will always be John Wood.

I suspected John Wood thought I was an idiot, at least partially confirmed on more than one occasion, the first time in class when I couldn't decide if I wanted to call something the "pinnacle of achievement" or the "ultimate achievement" and ended up calling it the "penultimate" achievement, which is nonsensical since *penultimate* means "next to last," something I knew at the time. John Wood called me at home, concerned about my use, wanting to make sure I knew what the word meant. I told him I did, but who knows if he believed me?

ChatGPT may hallucinate, but it would never make that kind of mistake, so even if it could think and feel, it would never be haunted across thirty years by such a memory.

Two and a half years after that incident, John Wood called the last paper I ever wrote for him in a class on the history of the novel *brilliant*. (It was not.) At the end-of-year gathering celebrating the graduating students, I read a silly little absurdist story about two farmers who take some poets who had come by the property looking for inspiration and plant them in the fields, then harvest their poems into a book that wins the Pulitzer Prize. I enjoyed seeing John Wood's face turn from red to purple as I made him laugh. He clapped me on the back afterward. "Brilliant!" he exclaimed.

John Wood passed away a good number of years ago, but he is alive in my memories. Whenever I see anyone from my graduate school cohort, we inevitably tell our favorite John Wood stories. You can ask ChatGPT to tell a story, but none of those stories belong to ChatGPT.

What I want to say about writing is that it is a fully embodied *experience*. When we do it, we are thinking and feeling. We are bringing our unique intelligences to the table and attempting to demonstrate them to the world, even when our intelligences don't seem too intelligent.

ChatGPT is the opposite, a literal averaging of intelligences, a featureless landscape of pattern-derived text.

Why have we declared this a marvel when there's an infinite supply of greater marvels all around us?

CHAPTER 5

Writing Is Thinking

In every book I've written about writing, every talk I give about writing, I start at the same place: "Writing is thinking."

Writing involves both the *expression* of an idea and the *exploration* of an idea—that is, when writing, you set out with an intention to say something, but as part of the attempt to capture an idea, the idea itself is altered through the thinking that happens as you consider your subject. Anyone who has written has experienced one of these mini-epiphanies that is unique to the way humans write. This will have happened dozens and dozens of times during the writing of this book. As just one example, at the conclusion of the chapter on automation in writing, I engage in an extended metaphor where I say that ChatGPT has shaken the foundation of the house we once thought secure and we are now standing in the street, surveying the cracks. Some folks want to abandon the house for a "castle in the sky" while I want to make the house "a dream home."

That metaphor appeared spontaneously while I was first drafting the chapter. Not only did the metaphor feel fresh, but it was the moment that I realized those who come at these issues of what writing means and how we should go about doing it are coming from a fundamentally different base of values from mine. I achieved a moment of empathy with a point of view I don't agree with. They see an incredible vision of the future. I'm more concerned with preserving what I think is important in the present.

We tend to think of writing as the act of assembling words, but it's a deeper experience than this. Words may be symbols, but they are not abstractions; they are the method by which we express our ideas. Lots of the writing students produce in school contexts is untethered from ideas, which is one of the reasons writing in school has become so alienating. Without an underlying idea, the words have no importance and very little genuine meaning.

When ChatGPT strings together its tokens in the form of syntax, it is not wrestling with an idea. It is arranging language. There is no intention behind the expression. There is no objective in mind other than each word makes sense next to what comes before and after it relative to the original prompt. It is a technical marvel that this process produces text that seems to be the product of thought, but we shouldn't confuse that process for the kind of thinking humans do.

The thinking we do when writing is often not linear or even explicable. In his stream-of-consciousness novel *Dr. Sax*, Jack Kerouac describes the task he has set himself as a writer:

> The other night I had a dream that I was sitting on the sidewalk on Moody Street, Pawtucketville, Lowell, Mass., with a pencil and paper in my hand saying to myself "describe the wrinkly tar of this sidewalk, also the iron pickets of Textile Institute, or the doorway where Lousy and you and G.J.'s always sittin' and don't stop to think of words when you do stop, just stop to think of the picture better—and let your mind off yourself in this work."

This is thinking by not thinking, by letting the mind wander. The goal is to experience the ineffable and then somehow bring it to life on the page. That we are able to achieve this through writing should be at least as marvel-worthy as the technical feats of generative AI large language models.

Some of my best "writing" happens while walking the dogs or in the twenty or so minutes before getting out of bed in the morning as my brain works on a problem while I'm half-asleep. Everyone has had the experience of walking away from a piece of writing, frustrated at their inability to capture the idea on the page, only to return to the task a day later and have a solution arrive as if by magic. This isn't magic; it's our subconscious working away while we're doing other things. No, we do not and may never fully understand the mechanisms of the full range of our cognition, but this doesn't stop us from recognizing that human thought is distinct from algorithm-produced syntax.

When some talk about the "basics" of writing, they often mean something like words, sentences, and paragraphs, the organizing units of syntax, the very elements that ChatGPT deploys in creating its simulations of writing. The synthetic text ChatGPT produces is convincing because we confuse those surface traits for genuine meaning, often imputing (particularly in education contexts) intelligence on text that is, by and large, as featureless and indistinct, though "correct" as possible. It's interesting that this correctness is conflated with intelligence, perhaps because it is identifiable, explicable, and easy to compare between texts, but this doesn't mean it is something we should necessarily *value*. In fact, it *isn't* something we value when we read. No one, save the most pedantic grammar specialists, reads a piece of writing and marvels at its correct placement of commas or lack of dangling modifiers. When we are compelled by something we've read, we are inevitably connecting to some deeper human thing.

Reducing good writing to correctness drains it of its humanity.

ChatGPT sentences are like alien invasion movies where the aliens arrive clad in convincing human suits, but eventually the hero, who knows something is up, latches on to an ear and pulls the skin suit free, revealing the lizard scales underneath—only in the case of ChatGPT, we would see a matrix of machine learning braided together.

If we consider writing as the fully embodied practice that it is, words and sentences are not the basics or base units of writing. To start writing, first you need an idea.

As I consider my own thought in the previous sentence, I realize this isn't quite true. It's not even a full-fledged idea that's the base unit of writing. It's something smaller. Let's call it a "notion." If an idea is the atom, the true building block of writing matter, consider the notion a subatomic particle, perhaps along with the "inkling," "sense," "suspicion," and "hunch." See how I've just illustrated the thing I'm talking about? My idea that the idea is the base unit of writing has been further complicated by my active thinking about my own idea.

Regardless, something occurs to the writer, and there is an impulse or energy suggesting that this notion can be explored and expressed through language. Only then do sentences come into play. Clearly, sentences are not the building blocks of writing if we are looking at writing through the lens of process.

I have yet to meet a writer who thinks in sentences. First, there is thought—be that an image, an idea, a notion, or whatever—and only then are there words. Often in writing, the final specifics of the words used to express the ideas and capture the thinking are the last part of the process. The ideas in the book you are reading will be very close to what I've put on the page at the end of my first draft (though several revisions will invariably continue to shape those ideas). However, the specific words used to express these ideas will change quite a bit, sometimes in subtle ways, sometimes in much larger ways when it becomes clear that the words do not capture the idea I'm wrestling with. (I just moved *however* from following *quite a bit* to the start of that string of clauses. Why? It seemed like the right thing to do.) More than once, my editor will make a marginal note along the lines of "What are you trying to say here?" and I will have to go back and find the proper language to express the idea that is already present (at least in my mind), but not sufficiently clear to the audience.

This process is not always good fun. Thomas Mann said, "A writer is a person for whom writing is more difficult than it is for other people," by which he meant that if you are going to truly write, you are required to engage in this struggle and it will not be easy. To write is to care about what has been written. The idea you are attempting to express may evade capture no matter how diligent the pursuit.

One of the lies of ChatGPT is that it makes writing look *easy* or, by extension, if we're writing well that it should feel easy. The speed with which the text unfurls down the screen suggests that it *must* be superior to humans because we can't achieve anything like it. But this speed is merely evidence that ChatGPT's output is not the by-product of thinking, and the specifics of the idea expressed by the text is immaterial to the task at hand. If there is an idea in the ChatGPT-produced text, it is an incidental by-product of the process, not an intentional outcome. The ChatGPT process is identical if you ask for a limerick about a toaster possessed by demons . . .

There once was a toaster possessed,
By demons, it couldn't digest.
It popped up some bread,
With flames, it turned red,
Toast from hell, it was surely the best!

. . . or an analysis of Kissinger's philosophy of realpolitik and its role in President Nixon's outreach to Communist China. (I won't bore you with that one; the limerick is much more fun.)

Writing is inevitably a process of discovery for the writer. One of the reasons I muster the gumption to write a book every so often is to gather a couple of years' worth of thinking across many smaller pieces into a cohesive whole so I can better understand what I have been exploring, idea-wise, over that period. There are many aspects of this book I have been thinking about for years, but the final form of the thought will not come into being until I write it in the book itself. And truthfully, even enshrining these ideas in a book will not put them to rest once and for all. This is why you will have a hard time finding writers who enjoy revisiting their previous work. The most common feeling is a compulsion to further revise those ideas, something not possible when the book's text is fixed.

Rebecca Solnit, author of more than twenty books, including *Men Explain Things to Me* and *A Paradise Built in Hell*, was asked for her feelings about ChatGPT and other LLMs after the revelation that her books had been part of a database of pirated texts that were used to train generative AI applications.[1]

> I'm a writer because I want to write. I don't want a machine to do it for me. I'm a writer because the process of writing is creative in what I do with language, but also in how I understand the subject. I often feel that I don't think hard enough about things until I have to write about them. Often my understanding changes in the process of writing. That's exciting for me. That's my own development, which, ideally, is somehow also something I can share with the readers.
>
> I'm engaging in thinking, and what is the point of handing the job of thinking itself over, of understanding something more deeply, seeing the pattern that underlies? Why would I want to give up that profound experience?

Where I would quibble with Solnit is on this notion of "handing the job of thinking itself over" because outsourcing text production to ChatGPT is not handing thinking over so much as abandoning thinking altogether. This, however, is exactly right: "I often feel that I don't think hard enough about things until I have to write about them. Often my understanding changes in the process of writing. That's exciting for me." It *is* exciting. It is why, despite Thomas Mann's lamentations about the difficulty of writing and the challenge of making a living through writing, there are still millions and millions of people who engage in this struggle on an ongoing basis. It is the difficulty of writing that makes it enormously satisfying.

Some of you may believe that this is all fine for professional writers who *want* to write and don't mind the struggle. What's wrong with others who do not enjoy this tedium finding relief in a tool that will do this thing that is unpleasant and difficult and not rewarding in the way writers seem to find it?

As we'll see in a later chapter, this is a healthy impulse that may indicate some writing really doesn't need to be done, but to abandon all writing to generative AI is to abandon thinking itself.

Of course, writing is not the *only* way we think, but it is a truly excellent way to think. The realm in which we think while we're writing is called the *rhetorical situation*, a concept that is illustrated by thousands of writing instructors across America every semester by drawing an equilateral triangle on the board and placing the words *message*, *audience*, and *purpose*, each at one point in the triangle. The illustration is meant to convey the equal importance of these elements and that altering one element will inevitably require changes in the others.

For example, because this is a book targeted toward general audiences, I am taking the time to illustrate and explain the concept of a rhetorical situation, a concept that may be unfamiliar to some of the people I am communicating with. If this book were solely intended for writing instructors, I would assume my audience knows what I'm talking about and move on.

When we write, we are conveying a message to a specific audience (with specific needs, attitudes, and knowledge) in order to achieve a specific purpose. In some cases, the purpose can be quite simple in theory—say, a set of instructions for a sequential task like changing the oil on a car—but then prove to be much more complicated in practice as the purpose intersects with the audience.

How mechanically inclined is this audience in general? What is their experience with car maintenance overall? What is their existing knowledge of appropriate terminology? A set of instructions for someone who can barely tell the difference between a flat-head and a Phillips-head screwdriver must be different from those for someone who has previous experience in this domain.

When the purpose becomes multifaceted and audience needs, attitudes, and knowledge may vary at the individual level, but the writing must work across these variations, the complexities and choices become infinite. Every moment I am working on this book, I am both shaping my ideas and considering my audience(s). My big-picture purpose is to be persuasive, but underneath this, I must also be informative, trustworthy, and entertaining; otherwise, people are not going to read my book.

These calculations when working inside a rhetorical situation are both constant and without definitive answers. They require human judgment and are beyond the capability of any large language model, no matter how powerful they may become. That's not quite right. It's not just beyond the capability of a large language model; it is something an LLM is entirely unconcerned with.

Here I am going on about how complex it is to think inside a rhetorical situation, but at the same time, I must acknowledge that it is not a particularly advanced skill for we humans, that in fact, it is innately human and can be done even by wee humans. The first writing I was ever asked to complete in first and second grade was situated in a fully realized rhetorical situation. Every Monday, Mrs. Craig would hand us large sheets of newsprint paper with blank space on the top and four lines for entering cursive text below. She asked us a question: "What did you do this weekend?"

Our audience was Mrs. Craig herself, who was either a wonderful performer or genuinely interested in what the first- and second-grade kids in her classroom had done that weekend. (I'm pretty sure it was the latter.) We were to write a sentence or two in the provided lines and then illustrate the events in the blank space above.

Because of those pesky and persistent fine motor coordination issues, I struggled with these assignments. But oh, I was happy to tell Mrs. Craig about what I'd done that weekend. My mother kept these for years, turning them over to me when she and my father moved out of the home I grew up in. The newsprint paper practically crumbled in my hands. It was fascinating to see who I was, what I was concerned with the first times I was asked to write.

Judging from the evidence, I tried to make my weekend news interesting, informative, and entertaining.

> *Saturday we went sledding and I hit my head. Ouch! I feel better now.*
>
> *We got a dog whois* [*sic*; it took me years to learn to correct this default language to "whose"] *name is Melvin. He is cute but he bites me too. Ouch!*

Apparently, I was working on a theme.

Telling Mrs. Craig about my weekend prepared me for third grade with Mrs. Goldman, when, for the first time, I learned that thinking clearly inside a rhetorical situation matters and that when we write, there are real stakes attached.

Writers of middling accomplishment are not superheroes, but if we were, this is my origin story, the moment I was bitten by a radioactive spider or blasted with gamma rays. To my knowledge, there was no radiation involved, but there was peanut butter and also jelly.

The ask from Mrs. Goldman was simple: *Write a list of instructions for making a peanut butter and jelly sandwich.*

I don't remember the doing of this part, but as I wrote out my list in my terrible handwriting, I assume I worked as diligently as I did on any other school assignment, which is to say not very. I still liked school at this point in my life, finding it a nice place to do a few things that seemed interesting, hang out with my friends, play with the class pet (a guinea pig), and once a year in the fall make peanut-and-caramel-covered apples on a stick, everything a kid could want from life.

After we finished with our writing, Mrs. Goldman produced the necessary fixings for making a peanut butter and jelly sandwich and then asked us to use those fixings while following our own directions to the letter. This is how I found myself knuckles-deep in a jar of Centrella-brand creamy peanut butter, because in my instructions I failed to indicate that you should use a knife to spread the peanut butter on the bread. I know these things happened not because I have some kind of eidetic memory but because there is a picture of me captured by Mrs. Goldman in the moment in my stylish red-and-black-checked flannel, hand shoved inside the jar, grinning. I use it as my avatar on my newsletter as a reminder.

In that moment, I am a young person having fun while learning about writing, experiencing a lesson I've never forgotten, that there is an intention and audience on the other side of things you write, so spending some time considering them before you start writing is only sensible.

We tend to view thinking as a solo activity, emblemized by Rodin's famous statue of *The Thinker* hunched over, fist on chin, absorbed in thought. But with writing, at some point, the thinking ends, and we uncurl ourselves and present the product of our thoughts to an audience.

This, then, is the act of thinking through writing, taking a turn into *communication*, a word that also conjures connections to other words like *community* and *communion*. Writing starts with a kind of communion between ourselves and our minds and ends when this communion is joined with others as an act of community. The intersection between authorial intention and what is received by the audience involves a constant exchange where the author attempts to transmit the idea to the audience with the greatest fidelity possible, but while doing so, the idea may shift, throwing both author and audience in a different direction. The writing is experienced, used, and thought about by others, who may decide to do some writing of their own in turn. It is an endless, recursive process, an ongoing conversation. Even in something like a journal or diary, where the writing is personal, the writer is engaging in reflective thinking that will shape their perceptions and identity and how they interact with the world. In this way, ultimately even this private act will impact others in the community.

In Mrs. Goldman's class, I learned that a failure to think of the impact of one's writing comes with consequences, that we must be responsible for our words, not only because they are ours but because they will impact the lives of others.

Cogito, ergo sum—"I think, therefore I am"—Descartes's famous declaration of his knowledge of his own existence. If writing is thinking—and it is—then it must be viewed as an act of our own becoming. In Mrs. Goldman's class that day, through writing, I first recognized my existence in the world, the possibility that I was an agent, responsible for himself and capable of having an impact on others.

It was a gift I've never forgotten.

CHAPTER 6

Writing Is Feeling

After every mass shooting in the United States, a weekly if not almost daily occurrence, you will read messages of sympathy and condolence from our nation's leaders and legislators—thoughts and prayers, thoughts and prayers.

Thoughts and prayers were offered after the killing of thirty-two on the campus of Virginia Tech in Blacksburg, Virginia. Thoughts and prayers after twenty-six (primarily children) were killed at an elementary school in Newtown, Connecticut. Thoughts and prayers after nine parishioners were murdered during Bible study at a church in Charleston, South Carolina. These thoughts and prayers were sent following the deaths of forty-nine people at an Orlando, Florida, nightclub and sixteen people attending an outdoor music festival in Las Vegas. When seventeen students were killed at Marjory Stoneman Douglas High School in Parkland, Florida, and nineteen students and two teachers were killed at an elementary school in Uvalde, Texas, thoughts and prayers were offered in response.

A synagogue in Pittsburgh, a church in Sutherland Springs, Texas, a supermarket in Buffalo, a Walmart in El Paso, a Fourth of July parade in Highland Park, Illinois. There are literally dozens (hundreds!) of other places where this will happen between the time this book is sent to the printers and you, the reader, will encounter these words.

I consider the impact (or lack thereof) of these offers of thoughts and prayers on the communities to which they are sent, and I can't help but consider, in the grand scheme of things, how meaningless words can be sometimes, and yet even these meaningless words carry significant emotional baggage.

I think about these events, the responses of the people with the power to change the conditions under which they happen, and I feel . . . sad, angry, frustrated. These are not mere abstractions. I was not feeling any of these things before I started writing the passage above. As a fully embodied process, writing is not only thinking, it is also feeling. We conjure emotion through our writing, both in ourselves and in the reader.

What happens when we divorce the necessity of feeling from the act of writing by outsourcing it to something like ChatGPT, which cannot think or feel?

In February of 2023, following a mass shooting at Michigan State University, where three students were killed and five others injured, staff at the Office of Equity, Diversity and Inclusion in the Peabody College of Education at Vanderbilt University used ChatGPT to help draft a statement of condolence. They acknowledged the use of ChatGPT at the bottom of the remarks.[1]

The institutional condolence email—an entity's version of thoughts and prayers—has been standardized into a kind of boilerplate, the writing version of going through the motions, so why not just let the synthetic text generator take a swing?

Maybe because outsourcing expression following tragedy to tools of automation is the kind of thing that happens in a faceless dystopia.

One Vanderbilt student who had a younger sister attending Michigan State criticized the choice to outsource the statement to ChatGPT, saying, "There is a sick and twisted irony to making a computer write your message about community and togetherness because you can't be bothered to reflect on it yourself."

Reflect is an interesting choice of words, suggesting a belief that part of the duties for administrative leaders at the institution is to take time to consider the potential impact of any communication before it is issued. Writing is communication. Writers are responsible for the impact of their words on the community.

The student's objection is essentially a call to pay attention to the rhetorical situation, particularly the needs of the audience in these moments. Even if, or perhaps particularly if, there is going to be no substantive responses to these types of tragedies, there should be at least some small psychic cost attached to the choice of inaction.

While reflecting is the act of reconsidering events of the past, to reflect also means to return something to its place of origin without absorbing it. In that sense, statements of thoughts and prayers following a mass shooting show significant evidence of reflection, just not the kind the student is asking for.

I am sympathetic to the challenges of working as a communications professional at an institution that is expected to comment on large-scale events. How do you find something meaningful to say when forced to comment on the unspeakable and when every syllable may be scrutinized, including by some who come to what you have to say with deliberate bad faith?

Colleges and universities are in the midst of yet another flare-up in the never-ending campus culture wars, so maybe defaulting to algorithmic boilerplate is a safe way to go.

Given what we know about ChatGPT as an aggregator and averager of the content on which it's been trained and the sheer number of these messages that have been put into the world, you will not be surprised to hear that it has no trouble producing a statement that would pass public muster, while simultaneously saying nothing of consequence.

> Prompt: Write a message of condolence and concern to a college campus community (Founders University) following a mass shooting in which thirteen people were killed, including a beloved professor (Dr. Moira Middleton) and the captain of the basketball team (Jenna Johnson).

This was the response, generated using the default ChatGPT interface (GPT-3.5), and the text is entirely unedited:

> Subject: Our Deepest Condolences and Support During These Difficult Times
>
> Dear Members of the Founders University Campus Community,
> It is with profound sadness and a heavy heart that we come

together to address the terrible tragedy that has befallen our beloved campus. On [Date], we witnessed a horrific act of violence that claimed the lives of thirteen individuals, including a cherished professor, Dr. Moira Middleton, and the captain of our basketball team, Jenna Johnson. We extend our deepest condolences to the families and friends of those who lost their lives, and to all of you who are mourning these incredible losses.

In the face of such unimaginable grief and pain, we want to express our unwavering support for each and every one of you. The impact of this tragedy reaches far and wide, and we understand the collective shock, sorrow, and anger that it has ignited within our community.

The loss of our esteemed professor, Dr. Moira Middleton, who was not only a dedicated educator but also a mentor and friend to so many, is an irreplaceable void in our academic family. Jenna Johnson, a beacon of leadership and inspiration, brought pride and unity to our campus through their athleticism and sportsmanship. Their absence leaves a void that will be felt for years to come.

During these dark hours, we encourage you to lean on one another for strength, comfort, and solace. Seek the support of the campus counselors, chaplains, and mental health professionals who are here to provide guidance and assistance. We must remember that our shared sorrow can be a source of strength as we come together to heal and rebuild.

In the coming days, we will hold gatherings and memorial services to honor the lives we have lost and to celebrate the indomitable spirit of our campus community. We will also engage in discussions about the ways we can come together to prevent such tragedies in the future.

> We pledge to work tirelessly to ensure that our campus remains a safe and nurturing environment, and to honor the memory of those we have lost through our collective efforts to promote unity, kindness, and understanding.
>
> Please know that you are not alone in your grief. We are here for you, and we will support one another as we navigate the challenges of this difficult journey toward healing and recovery.
>
> Once again, our hearts go out to the families and friends of those who lost their lives, and we extend our deepest sympathies to you all. Let us remember those we have lost with love, compassion, and a shared commitment to making our Founders University community stronger and more resilient in their memory.
>
> Sincerely,
> [Your Name]
> [Your Title]
> Founders University Campus Community

ChatGPT has unsurprisingly learned the lessons of "thoughts and prayers" well, how to employ euphemism to temper any genuine or meaningful personal expression, so the message washes over the audience with all the impact of a ripple through a bathtub. Language like "terrible tragedy," "horrific act of violence," "incredible losses," "unimaginable grief and pain," and "collective shock" has become pro forma in official responses to events of mass murder to the point that they are now the written equivalent of white noise washing over the audience without making a mark.

But now consider how inaccurate language written in the absence of feeling can be.

These "incredible losses" are actually quite credible, given the frequency with which they happen. The "grief and pain" are not only *not* unimaginable but experienced quite concretely and frequently. Extreme and yet also inchoate emotions like grief and loss are indeed exceedingly difficult to write about because they are experienced at a level so deep they have the potential to unmoor us from reality. Calling this "unimaginable" suggests it does not exist and we shouldn't bother even trying to understand. Deep down, this is a colossal failure of empathy given how real grief is for so many in these situations.

One potential consequence of the repetitive issuing of meaningless verbiage in the wake of tragedy is to make us inured to those tragedies. It seems impossible that something can be simultaneously unimaginable and yet also common, so we have these motions to go through in response. If we are going to resist this benumbing, we must be mindful that writing is feeling, and if nothing is felt when we are writing, we are missing an opportunity to connect to our own humanity.

I believe we should respect both the opportunity and responsibility of what it means to feel as we write.

In February of 2005, my father spent a couple of weeks doing one of his favorite things, schussing the runs of the Winter Park ski area in Colorado. He'd just turned sixty-four and had declared an intention to retire from a very successful legal career. He and my mother would travel and spend time in a second home in Winter

Park, while he would enjoy the fruits of being an éminence grise in the field of labor and employment law, continuing to get paid to dispense occasional wisdom without putting in the sixty-hour weeks that marked the bulk of his career. Nice work if you can get it, and thanks to those sixty-hour weeks, he could get it.

By November of 2005, my family was gathered in my father's hospice room in the final hours of his life at the end of a not-very-long, entirely unsuccessful, frequently painful bout with lung cancer that had metastasized throughout his body. He'd been medicated into unconsciousness since he'd entered hospice the day before, which was a blessing for all involved, particularly him.

As my family sat waiting for my father's inevitable final breaths, a woman with a harp came into the room saying that she was a student doing research on the effect of music on the pulse and respiration of unconscious, terminally ill patients. Would we let this woman with the harp play some music?

Why the hell not?

The woman with the harp leaned over my father, taking his pulse, before sitting down and tilting the harp into position. I am aware of all of the connotations of harps and angels in heaven, but none of that was on my mind in the moment. I don't know that I'd ever seen anyone play the harp before. It's a frankly ridiculous-looking instrument when you get right down to it. I play a little guitar, and I can't imagine how one would begin to tune something with so many strings. What was about to happen would be either awesome or absurd.

The woman played the harp and in a soft but strong voice sang a wordless melody to her own accompaniment. I do not know for how long. I recall no specifics of the music itself beyond that it was harp and voice in combination. I know that I tilted my head back in my seat, closed my eyes, and felt tears streaming down my face, though I don't know that I would call it *crying*. I don't recall making any noise or heaving with emotion. My breathing remained easy. When the woman stopped playing, the tears ceased. I was not the subject of this woman's experiment, but her harp and her voice did some good for me in that moment.

A couple of hours later, along with the rest of my family, I witnessed my father's last breath. He gasped, the capillaries on his shaved head, starved of oxygen, flushed from red to blue, and he was gone.

In the aftermath of my father's death, my predominant emotional state was marked by a void between myself and my emotions. My wife and I had just moved to Greenville, South Carolina, where she had started her first job as a veterinary specialist following her residency in small animal internal medicine, while I had hooked on to a non–tenure track teaching gig at Clemson University and did my writing and editing. I went back to work a week after my father's death, a day after the memorial service, where I delivered one of the eulogies. Others attested to my father's character, his success as a lawyer and mentor to other lawyers, so I spoke about how he had been the inventor of the television remote control, which involved us watching TV together and him saying, "John, change it to channel seven." Big laughs in the Village Church of Northbrook, Illinois. It felt good to write and then deliver those jokes.

Back home, I would find myself simultaneously in front of the classroom, doing all the required parts of teaching a class, while also standing at a remove from these acts wondering how and why I was doing them, asking if the guy doing them was somehow unaware that his father had just died.

With hindsight, I have come to realize this is the experience of genuine grief, something I'd known only vicariously through books up to that point, making me a very lucky person by any measure, but as the pain of grief arrives for real, this is little solace. At first, it comes often, steadily escalating like a wave until it breaks over you before temporarily receding. Over time, if you are fortunate, the grief is more absent than present, and as you realize this, you occasionally even miss it, the companion you never quite cared for but got used to having around. If enough time passes, it may take the form of an echo, an almost welcome reminder of the person who mattered so much to you.

Every time I publish another book, I think of my father because I know he would've read it and wanted to talk about it.

Life goes on, and the moment with the woman and the harp and my family surrounding my dying father was filed away in the deep recesses of memory. In most cases, it would likely remain buried forever, except that five years after my father's death, as I was working on a novel with a main character who had nothing in common with me other than the fact that his father was dying of cancer, the scene I lived through returned, and I gave it to my fictional creation. The main character of the book (which would ultimately be published as *The Funny Man*) is a stand-up comedian, rich, famous, and on trial for murder. I have been none of these things, which is why I was interested in writing about this character in the first place, but as this character's father was dying, I realized that what happened to me—the harp, the singing, my father's last breath—also happened to him.

Writing that scene, five years on, I cried harder than I ever had at the time of my father's death. As I finished it, no more than a few hundred words on the page, I felt a combination of exhaustion and peace, the potency of which is difficult to describe, but which hindsight tells me was literal catharsis. All achieved through writing.

Perhaps I've convinced you that indeed, in matters of life and death, we should not outsource our expression to a chatbot that cannot feel (in addition to not being able to think), but even the most mundane writing occasions are opportunities for learning and benefiting from the experience of feeling as we write.

Consider a grocery list, a chore that any number of apps and smart technologies have attempted to automate so as to alleviate a burden from people managing this aspect of a busy household. But preparing these lists is an artifact of the knowledge we have and the care we extend to our families. I remember picking up a dropped list from the grocery store floor once, and among the items was *Pop-Tarts CHERRY* with *CHERRY* not only in all caps but underlined several times.

There is a story in that list, great feeling in those all-caps and underlines, and sure, for the most part, we produce these utilitarian texts without feeling much, but a few moments of reflection (there's that word again) reveal to me all the times that writing that seemed like a burden was, deep down, a kind of gift. Someone in that house needed cherry Pop-Tarts, not chocolate, not strawberry—cherry.

Here's another example, closer to my experience.

At times in my career, student recommendation letters have felt like the bane of my existence. The rhythms of the academic calendar mean they tend to come at bad times when lots of other work is happening. If you teach a lot of students, as I did, you may get a lot of requests. There is also the knowledge that, in many cases, the recipient of these letters will treat whatever is coming as pro forma. It is enough to know that a student could get a faculty member to write a letter; the specifics of what's in the letter matter much less.

Creating a generative AI–powered agent trained on my writing voice and potentially even loaded with access to the comments and feedback I've given students in the course of my work with them that could pump out good-enough recommendation letters in an instant sounds—to be 100 percent honest—kind of cool.

But it would be a mistake weighed against the benefits, to both me and the student, of engaging with the writing occasion through the lens of reflection and feeling. Years ago, uninspired by the pile of recommendations I had to produce, in order to defy the expected boilerplate of the genre, I made it my goal to tell a specific story about each student as part of the recommendation.

This choice forced me into my personal Wayback Machine as I'd try to conjure some meaningful moment that represented what I wanted to express about that person's abilities and character. Usually, it wasn't too tough, since I was often writing for students I was working with that semester. Other times, though, I had to dig through my digital archives of comments and assignments to bring the student back into focus. I don't have much of a memory for names, but I can recall specifics from essays or short stories I read more than ten years earlier, and once I remember the writing, I remember the person.

Soon enough, a story follows, and I can bring that student back to life on the page and hopefully convey something that will be interesting and impactful to the audience for the recommendation. But along with me remembering the student, something else is happening. I am also remembering the teacher I was for that student. Sometimes these memories bring forth feelings of regret or even shame as I recall past approaches that I now reject. I have yet to experience a course where I didn't wish I'd done something differently.

At the same time, I am reminded about the source of my pleasure in teaching, the chance to intersect with other individual, interesting lives, and perhaps when I'm at my best, to inspire them. Teaching is humble and often humbling work, but it is also awesome, the most fulfilling work I've ever done or will do. Writing the recommendations are a reminder of this, a reminder I would miss if I were to outsource this writing to generative AI.

When we remember that writing is an embodied process that invokes and involves feeling, we can better decide what writing still requires our involvement. Without all those writing experiences and their associated feelings, it is not an exaggeration to say that I would not be the same person today.

The arrival of ChatGPT changes nothing about the fact that writing *is* thinking, writing *is* feeling, and together, this thinking and feeling allows us to project ourselves into the world by communicating. This is not the work of bots.

It is the work of humans employing their writing practices.

CHAPTER 7

Writing Is a Practice

When my wife and I signed up for the HelloFresh home-delivery meal service, I had hoped that I might learn at least a little about how to cook.

I did not. There is a reason that services like HelloFresh, Purple Carrot, and Dinnerly are called *meal prep*, not *learn to cook*, and that reason is because being able to cook involves a *practice.*

So does writing, but let's start with my failure to improve as a chef during the six or so months a weekly box of ingredients was delivered to our door. The whole purpose of a meal-prep service is to make it more efficient and convenient to prepare satisfactory (or better) food at home. With preportioned ingredients and step-by-step instructions, any fool should be able to make a decent meal.

Not this fool, or at least not consistently. I was more than willing to follow the well-prepared, nicely illustrated instructions to the letter, but as soon as something unexpected happened during the process, an unstoppable spiral of failure would kick in. How hot is a pan that is supposed to be hot? What is the threshold between a simmer, a boil, and a vigorous boil?

Medium-high heat?

If I was told that it would take five to seven minutes to brown the onions and the onions were not brown, what am I supposed to do? Just wait a little longer? Turn up the heat? Move on anyway?

(I am half-convinced that there is some kind of cooking industry–wide conspiracy about how long it *really* takes to brown onions because not once in my life has it happened according to the prescribed time.)

The same problem would crop up when testing the doneness of meats and fish. I prefer my chicken moist, but I am also against harmful bacteria or, worse, parasites galloping through my insides, so I tended to cook the stuff to a texture of jerky just in case. Fortunately, my wife doesn't mind it a little (or a lot) dry.

I can't even talk about my attempts at sauces and the persistent problems of consistency and color. Some were thin as gruel, others gloppy like cottage cheese. None of them drizzled effortlessly over the finished meal in the manner suggested by the meal prep illustrations.

It's not like every last thing was inedible, and some of the recipes were pretty foolproof, but the experiment ended one evening when my wife looked at me and said, not unkindly, but clearly, "Do you really want to keep eating this stuff?" My answer was, "No." My HelloFresh attempts were a lot like ChatGPT's off-the-rack prose, something resembling the real thing, but also, undeniably not.

Cooking is not just following instructions on meal prep packages, it is a dynamic process with multiple factors intersecting in understandable but also infinitely variable ways. Cooking is a practice that consists of specific skills, knowledge, attitudes, and habits of mind. These dimensions of a practice are both discrete *and* work in combination with other parts of the practice. For example, using a knife to chop an ingredient into smaller bits is a fundamental skill that can be practiced independently, but for this skill of chopping to be truly useful, it must intersect with knowledge about what size and shape is best for the food to be chopped into for the desired outcome.

The wrist flip of a pan that turns the downside of an omelet up is a physical skill, but knowing when to employ that skill takes knowledge of when this can be effectively achieved, not to mention what temperature the pan must be heated to. A good chef has knowledge of ingredients, flavors, and different cooking techniques, but to apply this knowledge, they must be able to execute those techniques both through their skills, as well as attitudes like being creative, organized, driven, and of course resilient when the end result doesn't meet the goals of the original intention, and the only thing to do is try again.

When it comes to the habits of mind, a good chef can engage in both deductive and inductive reasoning. They must be able to go to the pantry and fridge and imagine how individual ingredients may combine into a satisfactory whole. They must also be able to taste a dish made by someone else and understand what combination of components and techniques resulted in that outcome or to evaluate one of those failures and know what went wrong so they can make it right.

Paul Hollywood of *The Great British Bake Off* is a baker, not a chef, but the same principles apply: baking is a practice. When he evaluates a contestant's effort as "over proofed," he's combining all the elements of his practice to draw a conclusion from the evidence, a Sherlock Holmes of pastry.

The practices of chefs and of writers are remarkably similar, something I believe to be flattering to both chefs and writers.

In terms of skills, writers must be able to conceive, draft, revise, and edit a piece of writing. They have to be able to make sentences that prove pleasing to the audience's sensibilities. The skill suggests they must also be able to analyze the needs of their audience, just as chefs are thinking about the tastes of their diners. Like chefs, writers must be able to think deductively and inductively, to look at the material they have to work with and craft a message, as well as to look at the messages of others and understand how and why they work.

For knowledge, writers have two realms they must be concerned with, their knowledge of writing as a process—essentially the ways writing works—*and* their knowledge of the subject matter they are writing about. This latter part of the equation is often the part that trips us up in school contexts, as we either allow surface-level syntactical fluency to stand in for genuine subject matter knowledge, *or* we confuse a student's understandable struggles with articulating an unfamiliar idea or concept—a problem of lack of knowledge—with a deficiency in writing skill.

In terms of attitudes, writers must be curious, open (but also skeptical), empathetic, and obsessive. They must be comfortable with ambiguity and complexity and oriented toward being both accurate in what they share of their own ideas and in how they convey the ideas of others. These are often hard things to do.

For example, in Chapter 1, it's fairly clear that my sympathies in terms of what large language models represent are with Gary Marcus and Emily Bender rather than Sam Altman and Geoffrey Hinton, but in order to maintain credibility, I have to be as fair as possible in presenting the points of view of Altman and Hinton.

For both chefs and writers, the overall efficacy of the practice is embodied in the end product—the meal or the piece of writing—and when the end product is successful, the process leading to that product becomes invisible. Talk about a paradox. A successful outcome for the receiver of the experience requires erasing the existence of the process that led to it, creating an illusion of, I don't know . . . genius? But ask any chef or any writer about that process, and they will tell you it does not feel like the act of a genius.

It is work, the purposeful work of building a practice.

It's a bit of a shame that writing, unlike cooking, is such a visibly uninteresting activity, largely confined inside the dimensions of the writer's own skull. There's no chance for a *Top Chef*–like show to increase the appreciation of what it means to engage in a full-fledged writing practice.

I think the fact that our writing practices are hidden from audiences is one of the reasons so many people so readily came to accept what ChatGPT is doing as "writing" as opposed to automated text production. Maybe it would help everyone understand more about the practice of writing if we acknowledged that just about anything can be understood through the lens of having a practice.

PRACTICES EVERYWHERE

Once you start to look at activities through the lens of practice, they are everywhere, and not just in the areas that we understand as being organized around overt practices like lawyers or doctors. Teaching is a practice, musicians have practices, athletes have practices. When we do work related to our roles, we are literally practicing our practices.

When the air-conditioning unit in our house conked out not long after we'd moved in, the technicians tasked with replacing it said it was clear the old unit in the attic had been installed before a bunch of other things that were now in the way and this was going to be a "tricky" one. There's nothing a homeowner loves to hear more than that an already expensive repair is going to be "tricky."

As the installation was happening almost directly above my head while I worked in my home office, I became intimately acquainted with how skilled HVAC installers employ their practice.

An HVAC installer goes through hours of training and certification, but there was nothing specific in the training or certification about this specific issue. It was a problem to be solved using the practice the lead technician had gained over a decade plus of doing the work. (I asked.) The company always paired a newer tech with an experienced one so someday, when the newer tech had assumed the senior position and they encountered a similar (though invariably also different) problem, they were prepared to solve it. The ultimate solution involved a reciprocating saw employed on the deceased unit. The lead technician warned me before he started, "This could get ugly." I was grateful for my noise-canceling headphones.

After they'd finished, the lead installer said, "That was a fun one" in a way that sounded simultaneously sarcastic and sincere.

It was a tough job, but I never detected any panic. The lead installer's experience made the chances of success nearly certain. But what is it about experience that translates into expertise at one's practice?

MORE THAN JUST TEN THOUSAND HOURS

I am trying and failing to come up with anything that has done more damage to how we think about and understand performance than Malcolm Gladwell's 10,000-Hour Rule. This "rule," shared in Gladwell's bestseller *Outliers: The Story of Success*, is derived from a selective reading of research by Swedish psychologist K. Anders Ericsson, in which he observed that the violin students at a German music conservatory who had amassed ten thousand hours of practice by the time they turned twenty years old had accomplished more than peers with less practice. This is a positive correlation, but as we well know, correlation does not equal causation.

Gladwell decided, unilaterally, and in the interests of delivering a pithy and palatable narrative, that this was a rule. It is not. Gladwell's massive success as a purveyor of big-picture ideas is a testament to his understanding of audience desires for clear explanations for how the world operates. Unfortunately, Gladwell's lack of care with nuance and fidelity to accuracy makes for a lot of bad information that morphs into folk wisdom, but which is not true.

The 10,000-Hour Rule has been debunked repeatedly, including by Ericsson himself, who declared that Gladwell got the research wrong, and "there's nothing magical or special about ten thousand hours."[1] A meta-analysis across a number of different activities found little correlation between the amount of practice and the effect of practice, including only a 4 percent correlation in educational activities and a 1 percent correlation in professional activities.[2]

Obviously, you can't improve at something you never do, and we all have to practice our practices, but the amount of time spent by itself is not a meaningful gauge of how one advances their abilities.

There's another trendy theory, particularly in education, that also doesn't explain how we improve at our practices.

NOT JUST GRIT

Another briefly faddish notion about the key to improved performance was packaged in Penn professor of psychology Angela Duckworth's *Grit: The Power of Passion and Perseverance*. Duckworth identified grit as the key to achievement, defining grit as "passion and perseverance for very long-term goals. Grit is having stamina. Grit is sticking with your future, day in, day out, not just for the week, not just for the month, but for years, and working really hard to make that future a reality. Grit is living life like it's a marathon, not a sprint."[3]

Duckworth illustrated the principle via the actor Will Smith, who remarked on his own work ethic in an interview. "The only thing that I see that is distinctively different about me, is that I'm not afraid to die on a treadmill. You might have more talent than me, you might be smarter than me, but we get on the treadmill together, right, there's two things: You're getting off first, or I'm going to die."

In her research, Duckworth discovered that almost regardless of subject and activity, those who adopt and apply this attitude have more success than others, which makes sense because if you would rather die than quit, you are going to achieve some things.

This is an appealing notion for those tasked with achieving equity and providing opportunity who aren't inclined to consider structural barriers to achievement. Never mind disadvantages at the start, if we can simply teach people—particularly students—to be grittier, everything will fall into place.

Unfortunately, there are a couple of flaws in the theory. For one, following the example of Will Smith, it strikes me as unsustainable to expect everyone to work themselves to the brink of death in order to achieve success. Taken literally, Smith's approach would mean that the very grittiest individuals are the most likely to perish.

For two, as Duckworth herself freely and repeatedly states, we don't know how to teach grit.

More unfortunately, this did not stop a series of California school districts from testing students on grit-related measurements like "self-control" and "conscientiousness"[4] and then using these measurements to judge the effectiveness of teachers and schools. To her credit, Duckworth seemed to view this as her monster-escaping-the-lab moment, telling the *New York Times*, "I don't think we should be doing this; it is a bad idea."

In an op-ed commentary on attempts like the one in California to inculcate grit in students and then correlate that with the effectiveness of teachers, Duckworth remarked, "We're nowhere near ready—and perhaps never will be—to use feedback on character as a metric for judging the effectiveness of teachers and schools. We shouldn't be punishing schools for how students perform on these measures."[5]

Grit is an appealing notion, and those among us who are naturally gritty will swear by its efficacy, but grit as a pure source of drive appears to be more like a naturally occurring personality trait—like being introverted—rather than a mindset that can be cultivated through deliberate practice.

We need to look elsewhere to understand how to improve our practices.

"ONE KEY THING"

The 10,000-Hour Rule and Duckworth's grit theory are manifestations of a particularly American attitude toward self-improvement that a better life is right around the corner if you can simply identify and embrace "one key thing." This attitude dominates fitness and wellness spaces as we're informed of the optimum diets and workouts. Businesses chase one fad after another in the pursuit of increased employee productivity and profits. It's not incidental that the business and self-help sections in the bookstore are virtually indistinguishable when it comes to the prevalence of books that promise to "unlock the keys to success" with this "one simple rule/tool/principle."

The early stages of the AI gold rush bear similar hallmarks, as opportunists promising routes to unlock the secrets of your company's data by adding in the secret sauce of generative AI are everywhere.

Schools have been subjected to waves of educational fads to the point where Duckworth's grit is a tiny blip along the timeline of interventions that were supposed to help all children succeed.

Believing that there is "one key thing" and falling for the repeated promises of those who sell such remedies is a natural outgrowth of not wanting to deal with the inevitable complexity of operating in the world as it actually is. Some of the enthusiasm for ChatGPT seems related to these mindsets. We agree that writing is time-consuming, difficult, and often unrewarding, so having a robot assistant that can do it for you is incredibly seductive. It *would* be awesome to wash away the pain and angst that attaches to the writing we do in work, school, and life.

But to believe this requires us to conflate writing with automated syntax generation. These are not the same.

There is some truth in these keys to success, like engaging in ten thousand hours of practice or adopting a gritty mindset, but the reality of how we improve at our individual practices is that we must practice our practices in ways that directly engage the development of the four dimensions of any practice, those skills, attitudes, knowledge, and habits of mind.

FINDING FIT, NOT GRIT

Adam Grant, a Wharton School–based organizational psychologist, is far too positive a public person to say so, but in some ways, I feel as though his 2023 book, *Hidden Potential: The Science of Achieving Greater Things*, was written specifically to bury the 10,000-Hour Rule and grit as popular or prevailing theories of human development.

So, according to the raft of research and examples Grant has mustered for his book, what does matter when it comes to improving our practices? We benefit from three big principles: making sure practice is purposeful, varied, and fun. Essentially, we develop best when we ignore that we're trying to get better at something and instead just do a bunch of stuff that's related to our big-picture goal. Our orientation should be around finding the best fit for our interests rather than relying on grit because that fit makes it much easier to be gritty.

One key to finding our fit? Running away from boredom.

In *Hidden Potential*, Grant illustrates these principles through the example of the NBA's Steph Curry, a lightly regarded college recruit with questionable physical gifts (by NBA standards anyway) who turned himself into a generational superstar by embracing the principle of, in the words of Curry's trainer, Brandon Payne, making sure there's "no boring in our workouts."[6] Curry's individual workouts take the form of games where he challenges himself to score a certain number of points in a set period of time through a combination of layups (one point), two-point shots, and three-point shots, during which he has to sprint to the middle of the court in between each shot, building stamina in the process. During practice and before games, Curry does a series of trick shots that one would never purposefully attempt in a game, but the novelty and difficulty of the challenge makes the only semi-impossible shots he attempts in games seem relatively easy.

As Grant notes, "The variety isn't just motivating—it's also better for learning. Hundreds of experiments show that people improve faster when they alternate between different skills."[7]

The chance to experiment and find fit seems to have largely disappeared in school contexts as the aperture through which students are expected to pass on the way to success has become increasingly narrow during the current era of education standardization.

I do not think that Mrs. Goldman, my third-grade teacher, was necessarily fully versed on the social science research Grant covers in *Hidden Potential*, probably because much of what Grant cites hadn't been produced yet, but the spirit of play infused her approach, and it is that spirit that resulted in the writer origin story I shared earlier.

Imagine the violinists K. Anders Ericsson studied relentlessly sawing away at the same scales over and over for ten thousand hours and expecting that they would emerge concert-ready. This is how writing is experienced by the vast majority of students in American school systems, an experience that then colors attitudes about writing and makes it much more difficult to begin to forge a robust writing practice.

I believe ChatGPT is viewed as a desirable alternative because, sadly, most people have not been given the chance to explore and play within the world of writing. We have taken something that is dynamic, useful, and uniquely human and turned it into a series of rote exercises with limited or even absent purpose. This is true whether we're talking about school, work, or otherwise.

It doesn't need to be this way. Everyone can better understand what and how they write as being situated inside a writing practice. And once you have a writing practice, you may surprise yourself about what you're capable of.

I only wish someone had informed me of my writing practice much earlier.

CHAPTER 8

Life with a Writing Practice

I was very late to recognize I had such a thing as a writing practice, which is a shame because it's what has made my professional life as a writer possible. Someone should have told me, which is why I'm going to tell my story to you all.

The story starts with a man named Leo who made me cry . . . twice.

The first time Leo made me cry was the first time I met him in a job interview I was not properly prepared for.

This was six or so months after I had finished my graduate studies in creative writing and English literature, a dual MFA/MA program. I'd spent three years at McNeese State University in Lake Charles, Louisiana, banging my head against the challenge of improving as a creative writer, having only limited success, at least as I perceived things. When this ended, having no prospects for a career as a writer, I found myself in the basement of my parents' house because they had downsized over the years, not planning on having a broke, prospect-less twenty-seven-year-old back under their roof.

Nevertheless, I was lucky to have parents with a basement in which to land. Luckier still was my mother scoring a ghostwriting gig for me when she ran into a former customer from her bookstore who had a niche as a temporary CEO/CFO for corporations in post-bankruptcy declaration turnaround. He wanted help putting together a book on his business philosophy, and him being a frugal manager by nature and me claiming to know something about both writing and how to lay out a document in PageMaker (both mostly true), we struck a deal.

When I completed the project, two things happened. One, I used the money to move into a basement of my own, a small "garden" apartment near Wrigley Field. It was a terrible place, but it was mine. The second thing was that my ghostwriting client had arranged for me to meet "Leo." I was told nothing about Leo other than he worked in market research, whatever that was.

The commercial internet was not yet available. Google was still just a large number, not a place to go for answers to any question. Today, ChatGPT will generate a semi-accurate biography of Leo J. Shapiro in an instant. I knew I was ignorant, but there wasn't much I could do about it.

On the appointed day, I found myself outside the appropriate suite in the North Pier area of Chicago and saw that, on the door, it said, *Leo J. Shapiro and Associates.* As a master of deduction,

I realized that Leo was likely to be an important person at this place given that it appeared to be named after him.

As I discovered later, Leo was a giant in market research, famously blunt and irascible, but rarely wrong. He was most famous for designing the research that proved disposable diapers would be a big hit for client Kimberly-Clark. He was profiled in the *Wall Street Journal* at his passing in 2016 at the age of ninety-four.[1]

I handed Leo one of my résumés, and his face took on a mild look of disgust before speaking. "So, David says you're someone I should talk to, but looking at this"—here, he sort of swished the paper back and forth under his fingers across the table—"I'm having a hard time seeing why."

It got worse from there. I don't remember many of my answers to Leo's questions, but trust that they were mewling and unremarkable. One thing I do remember very vividly is, at one point, Leo looking again at my résumé and saying, "Why would anyone go to school to learn to write? Hemingway went to war."

"Well," I replied, "there wasn't one going on at the time." Leo looked at me with what I took as some mixture of pity and disgust over my ignorance.

"Son, there's always a war going on somewhere. Hemingway went to Spain."

"I hear Spain is nice," I replied, wishing I could melt through the floor. (I didn't actually say that, but it would've been funny if I had. The stuff prior to that is very close to verbatim because I went home and wrote about it afterward.)

Immediately upon leaving the building, feeling the distress over a failed interview, I went to the 7-Eleven next door, bought a forty-ounce bottle of malt liquor, and, leaving it in the paper bag, cracked it open and proceeded to walk the four or so miles along the Chicago lakefront back to my crappy basement apartment I wouldn't be able to afford much longer, tears of frustration welling in my eyes.

I had internalized every last widely held public notion of the uselessness of an English degree, and here I was with three of them and a person of authority confirming my worst fears.

Feeling the effects of that first malt liquor and perhaps some additional alcoholic beverages intended to drown my sorrows, I was awakened the next morning by a call to my apartment phone from a woman named Sara at Leo J. Shapiro and Associates who informed me that Leo said I should come in and see if they could put me to work, and how about tomorrow?

Maybe not melting down in front of Leo was the sole criteria for getting the job. I still couldn't say.

Once on the job, it seemed as though I was useful. Part of my early duties was to handle some of the overflow on word processing and producing presentations—this was the very earliest days of mass adoption of PowerPoint—and I seemed to have a feel for how to make the documents better aligned with the needs of the audience.

One night, I was asked to stay late so I could take notes for a focus group. Once I'd taken the notes, Daryl Gilbert, the moderator/lead researcher, asked if I wanted to take a stab at writing a draft of the report, something that normally she would have to do.

Why not? This task proved to be remarkably familiar and easy, essentially an exercise in sharing verbatim quotes and offering interpretation and analysis of the text's subtext, building toward an overall thesis. I had been doing versions of this since middle school language arts class. I gave my draft to Daryl, and forty-five minutes later, she pinged my cubicle phone and asked me to come into her office and to close the door behind me. Still skittish about my prospects, I was certain I'd missed some nuances of the form and was in trouble, but instead, Daryl exclaimed, "This is fantastic!" and then in a quieter voice, "Eventually, I'll have to spread you around, but for now, you work for me."

This felt very good. It seemed clear that I had a set of skills that could be of some use in this area of qualitative research, and I would get to keep this job. Perhaps someday I would make enough money to even live aboveground!

I was moved to a better cubicle as other trainees—I later found out that's what I was—washed out of the company after failing to find their niches. Some of these trainees had arrived with relevant degrees like sociology and marketing from elite institutions like Northwestern and the University of Chicago, but *they* were not useful, while the possessor of three useless English degrees (from state schools, no less) was thriving. I wasn't above a little schadenfreude then, nor am I now.

And then probably about six months into my employment, spring 1998, my cubicle phone's caller ID lit up with Leo's extension. I'm not sure he'd even spoken to me since I started, and here I was being summoned into his office.

This is the second time he made me cry because he said this to me.

> *I need you to draft a questionnaire for a study for [an environmental nonprofit organization] investigating the overall*

> *attitudes and donation habits of both current donors and prospective donors with the purpose of uncovering information that will help [the organization] increase their revenue base.*

I went to the bathroom to cry—not for long! I did consider quitting—not for long! But yes, I had no idea how to do what Leo was asking me to do. Clearly, this was a test that once failed was going to separate me from my gainful employment. Not only would I not be moving aboveground, I would be lucky to hold on to my basement hovel.

I flashed to a previous time when I was asked to do something I had no idea how to do, another time I thought of quitting. This was my first semester of graduate school, where even though I was there to become a great fiction writer, I was required to take a course in the Form & Theory of Poetry, taught by our program's brilliant, eccentric, and demanding director, John Wood. A few weeks into the course, after we'd mostly been listening to and appreciating John Wood's erudition, he gave us an assignment.

> *You are to write an explication of a single poem discussing how language, imagery, and structure combine to help convey the poem's meaning. Eighteen to twenty pages should do.*

No one else in the class seemed all that fazed by the request, but at the time, it seemed impossible to me. I wasn't prepared to write twenty pages about anything, let alone a single poem.

I tried to work the problem, focusing on key questions:

- What is a poetry explication?
- What is the purpose of a poetry explication?
- Who is a poetry explication for?
- What does a poetry explication look like?

I borrowed examples from students who had previously taken the class, seeking answers to my questions. I chose a poem, Gerard Manley Hopkins's classic sonnet "God's Grandeur."

The world is charged with the grandeur of God.
It will flame out, like shining from shook foil;
It gathers to a greatness, like the ooze of oil
Crushed. Why do men then now not reck his rod?
Generations have trod, have trod, have trod;
And all is seared with trade, bleared, smeared with toil;
And wears man's smudge and share's man's smell: the soil
Is bare now, nor can foot feel, being shod
And for all this, nature is never spent;
There lives the dearest freshness deep down things;
And though the last lights off the black West wend
Oh, morning, at the brown bring eastward, springs—
Because the Holy Ghost over the bent
World broods with warm breast and with ah! bright wings.

I read this poem out loud to myself over and over until it was memorized. I attempted gesticulating as I read, like I'd seen John Wood do in class. It helped. All writing includes rhythm, poetry especially so, and marching around swinging your arms to the beat delivers a palpable experience of the words. Over time, I started to notice some things like how the single-syllable, equally stressed metrical feet of "have trod, have trod, have trod" actually sounds like trudging footsteps.

I noticed that at the very conclusion of the poem, "and with ah! bright wings." That exclamation point creates a kind of pause that signals a gathering of breath before the finish of "bright wings," which sounds like an ecstatic epiphany, as those *i* vowel sounds force your mouth open in an image of awe, appropriate given the theme of the poem as a literal tribute to the awesomeness of God.

My copy of the poem was fairly quickly covered in scribbles and arrows and notes. I made dozens of observations. From those observations, I started writing, and because writing is thinking, those observations started to combine into inferences, essentially mini-ideas. As the mini-ideas accrued, bigger pieces of analysis appeared. The words filled the pages and the ideas seemed to belong together, and before I knew it, I had a twenty-plus-page poetry explication.

Did the earth shatter at my insights? It did not, but it passed muster at a level that allowed me to hold on to my position in the program.

After getting past the shock of Leo's demand for a quantitative study questionnaire, I realized that I had a method to fall back on, the method I'd used for the poetry explication, the same method I'd used for that qualitative focus group report. I could look at examples of what I was expected to produce. I could make observations about the content that belonged inside this container. I could draw inferences from those observations to craft that content that fulfilled the demand of the rhetorical situation.

I did these things. I had never bothered to look at a questionnaire previously, but it became apparent that a questionnaire opens with questions meant to identify if these are the people we're supposed to talk to for the purposes of the study (what's known as a *screener*). I saw how the questionnaire was structured in sections and tended to move from general to specific queries. I saw how different scales (five-point, agree/disagree, etc.) could be employed depending on the type of question asked. I saw how open-ended questions were sometimes used as follow-ups. I saw that a good open-ended question had to be phrased in such a way to invite natural commentary as part of the flow of the questionnaire. This required me to understand the survey from the audience's point of view, something I became very good at and which helped me make my surveys as tight as possible, saving time and money.

I had studied none of this in college or graduate school. I'd never taken a course in research methods, marketing, or sociology. I had my three worthless English degrees, but somehow, I managed to write a fully fledged quantitative questionnaire, a sophisticated work product in a field I had not known existed six months earlier.

My studies of literature and writing had taught me how to think in an entirely different field.

This skill has allowed me to forge a varied and frankly enjoyable career essentially doing whatever it is that comes across my radar by trusting in my writing practice and believing I can figure things out. Short humor became a popular niche in the early days of the internet, and never having written anything funny before, I broke down how funny stuff seems to work and started writing that, leading to my first book.

I wanted to write a novel, so I figured out how novels work. I turned that novel into a screenplay (never produced, but still . . .) by studying other screenplays. I wrote about and reflected upon my work teaching writing and managed to become an acknowledged expert in how we teach writing despite having an extremely limited academic background in writing pedagogy.

As I signed the contract for this book, I took a deep breath, making sure I had the necessary breadth and depth of material to pull it off, and knew it was true, all because of my writing practice. It is a kind of freedom to be able to have confidence that I can figure stuff out for myself. Without writing, that never would have been possible. This is what I wish for students, and it is something that must be established independent of using large language models for text generation.

I well know that in terms of intellectual firepower, I'm reasonably armed, but not tremendously gifted. In my various travels, I have intersected with genuinely brilliant and uncommonly creative people, and I know I am not them. Unlike Will Smith, if you and I get on treadmills together, I will very willingly get off first, if that's important to you, because I don't want anyone to die. I am, happily, entirely ordinary in just about every way.

But I have my writing practice, and that matters.

CHAPTER 9

Reading and Writing

There would be no writing and no writing practice if first there were no reading.

I am very fortunate on the reading front. I was kept in a bassinet in the back office of my mom's bookstore as an infant. Once I was a bit older, and after the store expanded, I was allowed to sit in a reading booth in the children's section, any and every book in the section available to me, provided I was gentle enough that it could still be sold as new.

I was partial to sports biographies, the novels of Matt Christopher, Tintin and Asterix comics, Encyclopedia Brown, E. L. Konigsburg (*From the Mixed-Up Files of Mrs. Basil E. Frankweiler*), Beverly Cleary (*The Mouse and the Motorcycle*), Judy Blume, *The Dark Is Rising* series by Susan Cooper, *The Chronicles of Narnia* . . .

I was not a brave or adventurous kid, by any stretch, but it's fair to say that reading gave me access to the world.

I suppose it's a mistake to tell you that I was partial to anything because in truth, I was happy to read it all, graduating to adult books when I was not yet an adult, starting with relatively tame choices like the spy novels of Robert Ludlum and Frederick Forsyth, but also reading Jean M. Auel's *Clan of the Cave Bear*—a kind of neanderthal soap opera including sexual content I (thankfully) did not understand at the time.

Books have been my constant companions. I already own more unread books than I could ever read, and yet every week, I acquire more books. There is a Japanese word for this, *tsundoku*, a reference to literal piles of books waiting to be read. To me, these are comfort, not clutter.

The novelist Hilary Leichter describes reading as a "partnership" between reader and writer. "When a book arrives somewhere emotionally moving, it's because the reader has helped put it there."[1] Leichter is correct. Writing is communication within a community, and the circle is closed at the moment of reading. Because we are unique individuals, the potential results of these joinings are infinite. I find this astounding.

There is a passage at the end of the short story "A Father's Story" by Andre Dubus, a first-person narrative from the point of view of a Catholic man who believes in sin and hell—two concepts I personally find dubious—deciding to commit a grave act that he believes will consign him to an afterlife of torture in order to protect his daughter from serious consequences of her own mistake. The end of the story chokes me up every time, to the point where I had to stop teaching it because it was embarrassing to grow suddenly emotional in class.

I share none of that character's beliefs or background, and yet, for a moment, we are joined.

Again, astounding.

Proust, who was at heart a philosopher of reading, described the phenomenon this way: "Every reader finds himself. The writer's work is merely a kind of optical instrument that makes it possible for the reader to discern what, without this book, he would perhaps never have seen in himself."

Reading is thinking and feeling in all the same ways as writing. Reading is a process that allows us to better understand the world and one another, sometimes even achieving something like virtual or alternate reality in our own minds as we join with the thoughts of others. Forget Mark Zuckerberg's metaverse or Apple's Vision Pro virtual reality goggles. Reading is the equivalent of Spock's Vulcan mind meld.

It is an inherently intimate act. George Saunders said:

> I think that what any of us pays for when entering into a reading experience is that feeling of seeing another mind at work, and not at work in a rational way. There's something thrilling about seeing this other mind at work in this blissful and private and self-referential way, and then suddenly your mind joins it. How weird and inexplicable that is. There's a sort of knowledge that goes beyond our mundane everyday knowledge. The reader and writer are being smarter together than either one could be separately.

> This is like a sort of experiential proof of the fact that our apparent separation is delusional.

Saunders is invoking a common experience of deep reading, the epiphanic insight, where the mind of another triggers a previously unknown connection in our own, almost as though the idea was there waiting to be unearthed all along. This is akin to the aspect of writing as thinking when the act of writing alters the original idea. In this case, the reading is both precursor and corollary to the work of writing, like practicing one's jump shot before hoisting up a three-pointer in a game situation.

To a significant extent, because of my background, my work, my disposition, I cannot wholly separate myself from my reading. My reading *is* me.

Why do I share all these bona fides, testifying to my abiding love of the deep engagement of reading, my belief that books are almost miraculous in their ability to remove us from our present concerns and attune us to the perspectives of others?

Because ultimately, I'm going to confess to you when and why I've been letting GPT "read" for me. But not yet. First, we have to go even deeper on deep reading.

Maryanne Wolf is a professor and author of *Proust and the Squid: The Story and Science of the Reading Brain* and *Reader, Come Home: The Reading Brain in a Digital World*, two works on theorizing, historicizing, and then literally mapping—via neuroscientific studies—what happens when we read.

Wolf's books explore her significant concerns about us losing our reading abilities, or even worse, raising generations of kids who do not have access to the kinds of experiences that are uniquely available through deep reading.

There are several important aspects of reading, particularly deep reading, to consider before we look at the way a large language model "reads."

First, reading is not an innate biological function like speech. It is an adaptive behavior cobbling together the frontal, temporal, and parietal regions of the left hemisphere,[2] unlike speech, which is largely confined to a specific region.

Second, reading undergirds other aspects of our overall cognitive development around memory, critical thinking, and empathy, among other things. Reading invokes the brain's "plasticity," the ability to adapt to new challenges. Different kinds of reading develop different aspects of our reading brains.

Finally, and perhaps most importantly, digital texts are changing the way we read and appear to be threatening the skills of deep reading, the ability to be totally absorbed in a text. The challenges of concentrating on text are undermined by a culture where we are expected to spend much more time skimming and assimilating significant volumes of information than we are deeply considering the ideas and concepts in those texts. We should pause to recognize the irony of this when we have multiple tools, now including the large language model, that can be used to retrieve whatever information we wish on demand.

Even those of us inculcated to a culture and practice of deep reading cannot deny the deleterious effects of screens and digital text on our ability to concentrate. Wolf describes the challenges she had in rereading Hermann Hesse's *Magister Ludi* for the first time in many years, after years of exposure to reading on screens. Hesse had once been a touchstone for her own fascination with reading as "the quest for knowledge."[3] But rereading *Magister Ludi* proved a challenge. "It felt sluggish," Wolf remarked, "like creosote going across my cerebral hemispheres."

Over time, Wolf had to retrain herself to read Hesse, first starting by only reading for short periods a day, forcing herself to slow down and allow the "immersive" qualities of the text to take hold. All told, it took her a couple of weeks before she could get back the sense of deep reading she once took for granted, almost like an athlete rehabbing from injury.

This kind of relationship to reading is unfortunately foreign to increasing numbers of young people who have been subjected to a school curriculum in which they are primarily exposed to short texts or excerpts of longer ones and then asked the kind of surface-level questions that are appropriate to multiple-choice standardized assessments. Deep reading is largely absent from the student reading diet because it is harder to assess against the standards that have come to dominate the curriculum.

Texts become things from which to extract bits of information rather than something created with a deep, communicative purpose. These attitudes are not confined to schoolchildren. Prior to being disgraced and convicted of fraud as a cryptocurrency Ponzi schemer, Sam Bankman-Fried told a journalist who had expressed his own love of books that Bankman-Fried would "never read a book."

After the journalist reacted with surprise, Bankman-Fried elaborated, "I'm very skeptical of books. I don't want to say no book is ever worth reading, but I actually do believe something pretty close to that. I think, if you wrote a book, you fucked up, and it should have been a six-paragraph blog post."[4]

Writer and critic Maris Kreizman calls this the "bulletpointification" of books and believes it is endemic to a tech culture that fetishizes optimization. "It seems to me that there is a fundamental discrepancy between the way readers interact with books and the way the hack-your-brain tech community does. A wide swath of the ruling class sees books as data-intake vehicles for optimizing knowledge rather than, you know, things to intellectually engage with."[5]

Reading and writing are being disrupted by people who do not seem to understand what it means to read and write.

Wolf argues that abandoning deep reading has literal evolutionary implications, none of them good.

I can relate to Wolf's struggles. I've come to look forward to scheduled plane travel because it offers a few hours where I can immerse myself in a book guilt-free and without the potential distraction of a screen like my phone or laptop. Keeping up my reading practice requires a diligence akin to physical exercise where I try to set aside thirty or forty minutes after lunch to spend with a book that has no connection to some other work purpose, just to practice achieving immersion. This practice often slips into a short catnap during which whatever I've been reading rolls through my subconscious. I awake feeling better than any other time of the day.

When times are busy, I let that practice slide, and I can feel my reading conditioning slipping, which makes me anxious and irritable, and yet I often will not act to get back to my practice because there always seems to be something more urgent and compelling that I should be accessing.

This is where outsourcing some of my "reading" to ChatGPT may actually free me up for more time spent on the deep reading that is a unique capacity of human beings.

I should not have referred to ChatGPT as being capable of "reading," because in the same way we should not confuse the synthetic text production of GPT with the writing of humans, we should not describe ChatGPT as being capable of "reading." LLMs do not have embodied experiences, because they do not have bodies—or even minds, for that matter. To the extent that ChatGPT can mimic aesthetic response to text, it is a by-product of surface features, not deep engagement or connections. It cannot achieve any of the things that Proust, George Saunders, or Maryanne Wolf describe as being endemic to reading when humans do it. ChatGPT cannot *engage* with a text.

That said, ChatGPT and other equally powerful models are especially good *processors* of text, and sometimes, having a tool that can process a lot of text very quickly and mostly accurately can be useful as a substitute for some of the "reading" we are often required to do.

Prior to the arrival of large language models, Wolf posited that in the digital age, we must adopt a "biliterate brain," one that is both capable of the kind of skimming that characterizes reading the internet on screens and the deep reading that helps develop our critical thinking abilities. If the large language model is going to be useful in the realm of "reading," perhaps it is as an assistant whose job it is to monitor and sort digital texts, and being prepared to bring forth the most relevant information responsive to my specific request on demand.

ChatGPT can also work as a kind of memory aid that allows me to concentrate on the unique things I am capable of—like actual thinking—while leaving some aspects of "remembering" to the machine with infinite access to information.

For example, I read Maryanne Wolf's *Proust and the Squid* a couple of years after its 2007 release in anticipation of writing an essay about my life as a reader. The essay never came to fruition, but the book stuck with me more than most books because I found it interesting and insightful, a solid deep reading experience. As I started considering this chapter, I pulled it off my shelf to have it nearby as a reference. As much as I knew the general thrust of Wolf's thesis, the specifics were beyond the reach of my memory. I turned to ChatGPT and asked it to give me a summary of the key points in *Proust and the Squid*, and in thirty or so seconds, it coughed up a seven-point list correlated to the main subjects apparent in the table of contents, along with providing short blurbs on the content and ideas within each chapter.

Because I am well aware of the potential for large language models to make stuff up, I used ChatGPT's outline to help me target specific sections of the book itself, significantly shortening the time it would have taken me to skim the text looking for the information I needed. Once in the book, I found some of the notes I had taken in the margins on my first read, the deep reading responses that had been triggered more than fifteen years earlier.

Using a large language model like ChatGPT, which is capable of searching the internet on your behalf, is like having an on-demand generator of CliffsNotes for just about anything you can think of. The streamlined process for calling up a collection of potentially useful information is amazingly helpful in many different situations and is a use that will undoubtedly expand as more people experiment with the applications and as more applications built to specific purposes are released.

As long as we are mindful of the constant potential of a large language model to make stuff up and double-check its outputs against original sources, I could easily see a role for it as a text processor.

But it's also worth considering what happens, or rather doesn't happen, as part of this streamlined process. For one, I am choosing to substitute the algorithmic processing of a text for my own thinking. It's possible, more like probable, that my reading of a text would find different aspects of that text worthy of consideration and highlighting. In this case, I was working with a text I'd already digested through deep reading, but if it had been an unfamiliar text, I would've lost out on something important when it comes to integrating Wolf's ideas with my own.

In high school, CliffsNotes were a handy substitute when I did not want to read the book assigned in class. The occasional end run around the school experience probably isn't all that harmful, at least I have to hope so, given how often I employed various techniques to avoid schoolwork over the years. But at some point, if you have never experienced the alternative, the substitute appears to be the real thing.

The result is a kind of academic cosplay where you've dressed up a product in the trappings of an academic output, but the underlying process is entirely divorced from the genuine article.

Real-life cosplayers well understand that they are required to use their imaginations to fill in the experience. They know they are not medieval knights or superheroes. Students who have exclusively engaged in academic cosplay will have no reference point from which to understand how to produce original insight. They will literally not know how to think.

Information extracted from a text so it stands by itself is not communication. It is not the route to generating new ideas.

This technology may be useful as an adjunct to deep reading, but we must recognize that processing text is not the same as reading.

Only humans can read. Only humans can write.

Don't let anyone tell you otherwise.

PART | THREE

CHAPTER 10

Reading, Writing, and Robots

In February of 2024, OpenAI CEO Sam Altman tweeted that "OpenAI now generates 100 billion words per day. All people on Earth generate about 100 trillion words per day."[1]

Altman meant this as a sort of statement of triumph, part of a larger shock-and-awe campaign he was prosecuting at the time, in which he declared that OpenAI would need $7 trillion in funding in order to produce the AI computing chips that would allow for the fullest expression of OpenAI's intentions in developing artificial general intelligence.

To put that number in perspective, it is about the same as the entire market capitalization of Microsoft, Apple, and Alphabet (Google) at the time of Altman's declaration. It is more than one-quarter of the annual gross domestic product of the United

States and about the same as the annual GDP for the United Kingdom and Germany combined. In the words of Sasha Luccioni, who heads up the climate research arm of Hugging Face, a collective working on sustainable development of artificial intelligence, "The amount of natural resources that will be required is just mind-boggling."[2]

Seven trillion dollars is seven times more than the entire country spends annually on public K–12 education.

While there is little doubt that the capabilities of generative AI are significant, even groundbreaking, with more capabilities being added all the time, it is equally clear that *how* generative AI does these things is not the same as what happens when humans do these things. Altman sees a de facto improvement. I am not so sure. I believe these differences in process matter. After all, this is our planet, our lives, and Sam Altman's notion that humanity's highest calling is to see through the development of a godlike superintelligence should be viewed as radical, not visionary or innovative.

There is no wishing away AI at this point, meaning it must be grappled with and done so in a way that preserves our humanity.

Because of this, Part 3 will be necessarily exploratory and speculative, examining the possible futures for students, teachers, readers, workers, and writers in a world where ChatGPT exists.

Many of the initial forays of this technology into substantive work have been pretty haphazard and bad—the lawyer citing nonexistent cases, for example—but my assumption is that in many cases, at some point in the future, this technology will work quite well at what it's designed to do. This scares me more than the projects that flame out like one of Elon Musk's SpaceX rockets because my fear is that we will adopt practices without considering the long-term consequences of these shifts. In order to get underneath the future implications of this technology, we have to talk about *labor*, the work we do in the world that involves writing, and what that labor means to our lives.

Without a doubt, having an AI that can produce text will alter our relationship with the text that is produced and the work that surrounds that production. If we aren't careful, we will lose things that it turns out we need but might have a hard time getting back once they are lost.

Personally, I am not concerned about my labor as a writer. ChatGPT may be able to churn out a book-length manuscript of grammatically correct prose that may even have some surface-level coherence, but it cannot write *this* book. It is not privy to the experiences that have informed my point of view. It does not have a process that allows it to combine these experiences with research and critical thinking in order to form analytical conclusions. It cannot write.

I wish I could release all the versions of this book that existed prior to this one, along with notes on how and why the book evolved as my own thinking developed. ChatGPT doesn't have a writing and thinking process that distills ideas toward their ideal form. As long as readers continue to demand the genuine article, I'm not concerned.

But what if, in our fascination with the new and cutting edge, we lose touch with the genuine article? It happens. When I was a child, heavily influenced by the marketing that said Tang was the drink of astronauts, I would beg my mom to buy us Tang instead of orange juice. Tang is perfectly drinkable. It is much cheaper than orange juice and particularly convenient if you're ensconced inside a space capsule. Tang is still around, but it does not taste as good as orange juice, no matter how much you might wish it to be true. The speed and novelty of Tang ultimately lost out to orange juice, which maintains a market many, many times larger than its ersatz powdered cousin.

But what if you'd never had orange juice in the first place? You might not recognize the trade-offs of going with Tang. If you value cost, speed, and efficiency, Tang it is. But if taste and nutrition are the thing, orange juice is the superior choice.

Just in case my analogy is not clear, ChatGPT is or at least may be Tang. I don't think we want a world where all we have is Tang, but we may stumble into that reality before we recognize it's happening if we're not careful and thoughtful.

It is risky to make predictions when there are so many unknowns working in combination, and yet, numerous times in the coming chapters, I will be making what look like predictions. I consider them as something more like *possibilities* or perhaps *probabilities* based in a reading of the evidence at hand and an understanding of the structural forces at work. Consider them pieces of a conversation in which the world is invited to join with agreement, disagreement, or some measure of both. This kind of conversation is also something that ChatGPT cannot do.

As we begin this exploration, I want to introduce a way of thinking about generative AI that I've found useful as I consider the impact of the technology on our school, work, and writing lives. It comes from Jane Rosenzweig, the director of the Harvard College Writing Center. She asks, "To what problem is ChatGPT the solution?"

When we start to look at ChatGPT as a tool that will replace a teacher, or a journalist, or a writer, what *problem* is it actually solving? Is it an issue of quality, speed, efficiency, resource availability? What if ChatGPT is not genuinely solving a problem but is instead being used to paper over a problem in a way that will cause significantly worse problems down the line?

The only way out is through. It's possible that I will not like some of the answers to my own questions raised in Part 3. The big question in my mind is how deeply rooted the alienation from reading and writing as embodied human experiences has gotten. Maybe we've habituated ourselves to Tang, and orange juice, with its weird pulp and sharp taste, seems odd. My hope lies in the fact that the existing alienation is surely a state we would like to escape should we be shown a route toward engagement.

I wonder, what's going to happen?

CHAPTER 11

Here Come the Teaching Machines (Again)

Not long after the public release of ChatGPT, Sal Khan, founder of online tutoring resources company Khan Academy, announced the launch of Khanmigo, an experimental ChatGPT-enabled online tutor that he claimed would be capable of providing one-on-one tutoring, on demand, for any student.

In a TED Talk touting Khanmigo, Khan declared, "I think we're at the cusp of using AI for probably the biggest positive transformation that education has ever seen." Khan literally believes that artificial intelligence could "save" education.[1] Khan has actually been on the saving-education beat for well over a decade since his first TED Talk in 2011, when he promised that his Khan Academy instructional videos would allow students to "go at their own pace," making the classroom "more human."

With Khanmigo, Sal Khan has now apparently found the key to making the classroom more human, and that key is a machine.

Khan is merely the latest in a long line of men—and they are all men—who believe that the "problem" of teaching can be solved with a teaching machine.

The hubris serially on display regarding the intersection of technological change and teaching is perhaps best illustrated by this quote from a legendarily smart person, speaking in 1922: "I believe that the motion picture is destined to revolutionize our educational system, and that in a few years it will supplant largely, if not entirely, the use of textbooks."

That person was Thomas Edison, who was besotted with his own invention and was certain moving pictures could deliver educational materials much more efficiently than books. But as we've seen previously, reading is a much deeper experience than mere information transmission, and learning is more than being exposed to information. Edison was wrong.

The list of august persons who have been dashed against the shoals of big claims of pending educational revolution extends beyond Thomas Edison. Sidney Pressey, a distinguished professor of psychology at Ohio State University, spent large chunks of the 1920s and 1930s pursuing his vision for an "Automatic Teacher." Pressey's invention was not a teacher but rather a mechanized testing machine where students would be exposed to questions, they would select an answer from among multiple choices, and then be either rewarded or redirected. Pressey even envisioned students receiving candy for correct answers.

In the 1950s, B. F. Skinner, the godfather of behaviorism, was similarly obsessed with the creation of a teaching machine, convinced that children could better learn if they were simply treated like the pigeons he had used to test his theories on the importance of immediate feedback and reward. Skinner believed the delay between students providing evidence of their learning and the judgment of that evidence was unacceptable, and a teaching machine was the solution. Skinner touted the benefit of immediate feedback, self-paced learning, and the freeing of the teacher from the demands of "correction." The machine, much like Pressey's, was efficient and indefatigable, a mechanical multiple-choice testing box. Despite decades of attempts, Skinner's machine never caught on. Skinner blamed schools, teachers, even manufacturers for this failure, never considering that perhaps children are not the same as pigeons.

Less significant figures have taken similar cracks at the problem. In 2015, in an interview with NPR, Jose Ferreira, founder of education technology company Knewton, declared of his signature product, "We think of it like a robot tutor in the sky that can semi-read your mind and figure out what your strengths and weaknesses are, down to the percentile."

Jose Ferriera flushed more than $100 million in investment capital as the hype was exposed. Ultimately, Knewton was sold for pennies on the dollar to education publisher John Wiley & Sons and now has a zombie existence as third-rate courseware.[2]

The definitive history of the failure of teaching machines is Audrey Watters's 2021 book, *Teaching Machines: The History of*

Personalized Learning, and throughout her study, Watters shows that the "problem" the teaching machines are trying to solve is the inherent variability and messiness of learning. In order to circumvent these challenges, the student must be changed from a human into a product. Once students are a product, we can use our machines to shape them.

The teaching machines keep failing because humanity gets in the way. For the teaching machine to succeed, we will have to decide that some aspects of our humanity are unimportant or inherently flawed, leaving us better off if we're governed by the outputs desired by the machines.

Khan champions Khanmigo as "personalized education" in which students with access to an "artificially intelligent but amazing personalized tutor" will go from "average to exceptional." Khan believes that Khanmigo, powered by AI, will be able to coach a student in much the same way as a one-to-one personal tutor. Khan believes that if the machine knows what the student knows, it will be able to put the optimum bit of information or stimulus in front of them to help them solve the problem at hand and learn.

It would be nice if it were true, but to believe it means ignoring all the past failures, failures that weren't predicated on faulty technology but rather on mistaken notions of how we learn.

As Watters shows in *Teaching Machines*, Khan is hardly the first person to have this nearly exact vision for building a teaching machine. He was beaten to it by nearly seventy years by a guy named Simon Ramo.

In 1957, during the heat of the space race between the United States and the Soviet Union, Ramo posited that given the speed of advancement in terms of technology and automation, and the impending conquering of space, there was a "coming crisis of education" that was going to lead the US to fall behind its rivals.[3]

Ramo envisioned a totalizing approach, in which students would be "registered" into the system, after which a personalized, data-determined path would be followed and tracked using something called a *chargaplate*, which at the time was envisioned as something like the credit card imprint machines of days gone by.

Each student's day would involve some time with teachers, but would primarily be in "automated" "push button" classrooms, working with teaching machines optimized for learning subjects like trigonometry.

Ramo believed a student would be less likely to daydream with a machine than with a human teacher. The machines would be "adaptive." Teachers would benefit, according to Ramo, by having the drudgery handled by machines.

Ramo's description of his proposed teaching machine in 1957 is nearly identical to Sal Khan's in 2023:

> [Students would be] seated in front of a special machine, again with a special animated film and a keyboard, but he is now alone and he knows that this machine is much more interested in his individual requirements. It is already set up in consideration of his special needs. It is ready to go fast if he is fast, slow if he is slow. It will considerably repeat what he has missed before and will gloss over what he has proven he knows well. This machine

> continues the presentation of some principles and asks for answers to determine understandings. Based upon the student's immediate answer, it may repeat or go on to the next principle. With some hints and assistance by the lecturer in the movie, and with appropriate pauses (not accompanied by a commercial), the student is allowed a period for undisturbed contemplative thought before registering his answer.[4]

As Watters notes, while this vision of technology was positioned as an aid to teachers—Sidney Pressey claimed his automatic teacher would "leave the teacher more free for her most important work, for developing in her pupils' fine enthusiasms, clear thinking, and high ideals"[5]—the underlying goal was to either replace or marginalize the teacher in the classroom, to make them technicians subservient to the technology.

It is not coincidental that teaching was (and still is) a female-dominated profession, while the engineering boom of the 1950s and 1960s was almost exclusively the province of men. This disrespect for teaching rooted in mid-twentieth-century sexism continues to be manifested today as teachers are subjected to an ever-changing list of demands without being given the time and resources necessary to do the job.

The list of technological solutions to teaching that have been tried and failed are almost beyond counting. In addition to Pressey's, Skinner's, and Ferreira's machines, we can add other technologically mediated approaches, such as the One Laptop per Child initiative, which was supposed to put computers in the hands of millions of children for under one hundred dollars per unit and managed to waste millions of dollars. Or consider the massive open online course (MOOC) movement, of which Sebastian Thrun, founder of MOOC provider Udacity, told *Wired* magazine that in fifty years, there would be only ten higher education institutions in the world and Udacity had a "shot" at being one of them.[6] By the end of 2013, Thrun had "changed course," declaring his own company's MOOC offerings a "lousy product."[7]

IBM spent years and hundreds of millions of dollars trying to create a digital tutor off its Watson platform—the original super-intelligent computer—but they abandoned the attempt in 2017 after recognizing they could not cross the threshold to a truly useful product. The project's lead, former IBM researcher Satya Nitta, said, "We missed something important. At the heart of education, at the heart of any learning, is engagement."[8]

Nitta, who spent over half a decade tackling the problem of the robot tutor, says that even with large language models, one-on-one tutoring is "a terrible use of AI—and that remains today."

Khanmigo is built on the "engineering model of education," the model on which IBM's Watson experiment was predicated and the same model that resulted in one of the biggest failed experiments in education technology history.

Larry Berger, CEO of ed tech company Amplify, was once a believer of the "engineering model," which underpins these visions of teaching machines and animates Khanmigo as well.[9] Amplify was one of the biggest original ed tech bets on personalized learning and was bolstered in the early to mid-2010s by nearly $1 billion of investment from Rupert Murdoch's News Corp in its chase for a software version of a teaching machine housed on a proprietary laptop to be sold into schools across the country. With Amplify, Berger was poised to reinvent how students learned by following the engineering model, which breaks down to these steps:

1. Figure out what students need to learn. Berger calls this a "map."
2. Figure out what students already know so you can place them on the map, "where they know everything behind them, and in front of them is what they should learn next."
3. Assemble "learning objects" and task an algorithm with putting the proper object in front of a student at a given moment based on their position on the map.
4. Make the student use the learning object.
5. Measure what the student has learned following an encounter with the object.
6. Reorient the student on the map. If the student learned, they advance. If they didn't, "try something simpler."

Berger believed, "If the map, the assessments, and the library were used by millions of kids, then the algorithms would get smarter and smarter, and make better, more personalized choices about which things to put in front of which kids."

Even on its own terms, Berger's map analogy breaks down. He's not describing a map so much as a line or continuum on which the student is expected to move step by step. Berger's use of "ahead" and "behind" are not terms we use when we think about maps. With maps, we are surrounded by territory and can move 360 degrees. Berger's engineering model presumes that learning is sequential and only progresses, without the possibility for regression, and that individuals progress in highly similar ways. None of these things are true when we look at the variety of human experience and how we learn. It is especially untrue of writing.

Over time, Berger understood these complexities when it came to his attempts to personalize learning through software, and his faith in the engineering model eroded. "Here's the problem: The map doesn't exist, the measurement is impossible, and we have, collectively, built only 5% of the library."

Berger believes the assessments are bad at revealing what students know: "Our current precision would be like Google Maps trying to steer you home tonight using a GPS system that knows only that your location correlates highly with either Maryland or Virginia." This is a problem more complicated from a machine learning perspective than even self-driving cars—another inevitable development that has failed to materialize.

It is possible that generative AI could significantly speed up the development of Berger's map, but even if this is possible, it does not solve the core problem of the engineering model and indeed any teaching machine, the problem that stopped Satya Nitta's experiments dead. As Berger says, "Just because the algorithms want a kid to learn the next thing doesn't mean that a real kid actually wants to learn that thing."

After a significant deflation in value, Berger reclaimed control of Amplify and pivoted to developing software that supports classroom activities, rather than attempting to replace teachers with algorithms.

Dan Meyer, a former math educator and a critic of the engineering model who now works at Amplify as the head of research, describes the digital-first tutor as "learning alone with laptops within social spaces like classrooms" and observes that, quite frankly, students hate it, for good reason. "That learning fails to answer their questions about their social identity. It contributes to their feelings of alienation and disbelonging."[10]

Sal Khan may believe that his program allows students to "move at their own pace," but it's just a bunch of individuals trudging toward the same destination. In reality, we should call these approaches to personalized learning *depersonalized learning.*

The engineering model is favored by those who are in the business of selling teaching machines because it is an approach that machines can accomplish. But students are not products, and teaching is far more sophisticated than what can be achieved under the engineering model.

The people who believe in teaching machines rarely evince any real understanding of what it means to teach and to learn.

Teaching, like writing, involves a practice, a combination of skills, attitudes, knowledge, and habits of mind. It is also a "wicked problem" where, even though we know quite a bit about what makes for effective teaching, the sheer number of variables at play and the inevitable wild cards of human behavior mean that constant adjustments are necessary.

Over the twenty-plus years I've been teaching or working with teachers, I've been consistently humbled by seeing my best-laid plans wrecked by seemingly the smallest possible difference, a butterfly flapping its wings that manages to change the direction of a class. I had numerous semesters where I would teach the exact same course—same curriculum, same types of students, same instructor (me)—literally back-to-back-to-back three periods in a row, and I would see marked differences in student response and performance.

Teaching is very difficult to do well, and when I started as a graduate student, teaching developmental English courses, despite doing the best I could, I was very bad. I sometimes fantasize about finding those students and apologizing. Over the years, I got much better, thanks to practicing my practice, engaging in a kind of never-ending experiment of trial and error rooted in a constant process of data collection.

I suppose it is unintentional, but Sal Khan's pitch for his all-knowing, indefatigable tutor is underpinned by a lack of respect for teachers and teaching. Learning is not about progressing along a continuum or even moving around a map. It is exploring in three dimensions. As a teacher, I have to be prepared for a student to zoom off in an *infinite* number of possible directions. Students are not static. The world changes as well. The idea that we could engineer our way into a universal best method for learning via algorithmic exchange requires a willful delusion about the world. While many patterns of teaching repeat, I have yet to experience a semester without some number of surprises requiring adjustment.

This is particularly true of writing. For one, when seen as a practice, we can understand how different aspects of the practice may develop at different rates and in different ways from person to person. Even when we can identify a definitive error in a piece of writing that's shared across multiple students, the origin of that error may still be different.

Imagine a very common mistake by the first-year college students I've primarily worked with, a failure to properly identify and then summarize the claims being made by another writer. Summarizing claims is a fundamental building block of writing inside the academic conversation, the exchange of ideas meant to shed additional light on a subject at hand. Failure to properly summarize a claim not only fails to add illumination, it points the light in the wrong place, so I try to make sure doing this is second nature for students.

An incorrect argument paraphrase can be rooted in any number of different issues. It could be a reading problem, as in the student didn't read, didn't read carefully enough, or lacks the necessary background to interpret the original message. It could be a disconnect between what I want and what students think I want based on previous expectations in their writing courses.

For example, early in the semester, rather than summarizing claims, which requires paraphrase, students, working from previous patterns of schooling, are more likely to simply describe the content of an article, such as:

> *In the chapter excerpt from his book* More Than Words, *John Warner writes about teaching machines and generative artificial intelligence.* (summarizing content)

versus

> *In the chapter excerpt from his book* More Than Words, *John Warner claims that generative AI as used in education*

> *is likely to become another example of a failed teaching machine, such as B. F. Skinner's "teaching machine" from the 1950s.* (paraphrasing a central claim)

It is very easy to detect this difference in student writing. I can do it at a glance, and ChatGPT could be prompted to do the same rather easily. Identification of the phenomenon, a surface-level indicator, is easy. Some people—many people—will be satisfied with an AI tutor that can do this easy thing, provide feedback such as "Make sure to share the author's claims rather than just summarizing content."

But ChatGPT is not reading this writing. It is responding to patterns of syntax.

This is not teaching. Once the disconnect has been identified, it's now my job to identify the root of the issue and help students go back to the well to make another attempt at the same skill.

Even with two decades of experience reading and responding to student writing, however, absent a conversation with the student, I am still only guessing as to the underlying cause of a deficiency and what steps should be taken to remedy this at the writing-practice level. This is why when I identify an issue with a student's writing, I offer comments that attempt to engage the student at the level of their practice in order to diagnose and remedy the issue that led them to an incorrect argument paraphrase.

This involves establishing trust and communication. It is significantly helped by motivating students through intrinsic rewards after having established a shared context and system of values that inform the work of the course. Creating the right atmosphere for learning matters as much as anything. It allows me to respond to students as individuals based on all the contextual clues I'm receiving.

In a given day, teachers make upward of a thousand decisions, and many of those decisions are reached through nonverbal context clues. Innumerable times I have been working with a student where I ask them if they understand what I'm saying and what they should be doing, and they say, "Yes," but their body language is telling me, "No," and we keep at it.

The engineering model of personalized learning assumes these moments of shared struggle simply do not matter, because it is the student who is on the march toward proficiency.

This is not true. In my courses, at the outset, I say that as a class, we are engaged in a "shared inquiry into the subject at hand." The goal is to have deep and rich experiences that spur students toward the kind of practicing of their practices that allows them to explore freely rather than move along a pre-mapped line.

This *can* be a real struggle, but that shared struggle is at the center of learning.

Next, we're going to explore what that struggle should look like in a writing classroom.

CHAPTER 12

Writing in the Classroom of Today (and Tomorrow)

When Daniel Herman declared that ChatGPT would be the end of high school English, what he meant is that students would find it irresistible as a way to submit assignments without doing any work.

This is commonly known as *cheating*.

Students attempting to do an end run around schoolwork is nothing new, whether by cheating or doing the bare minimum necessary to meet the requirement to check a box. If my literature class was going to test me on material in the CliffsNotes, why read the book? If I could skip a class in college—and I skipped many classes in college—and still get a decent grade, why would I go to class?

In a situation where the outcome is valued more than the process, a shortcut to the desired outcome will always be attractive. The chief innovation of ChatGPT on this front is its speed and accessibility. Having someone else write your school essay has always been an option, but it would take time and/or cost a few bucks. Now, that output is just a prompt and click away.

It has been and will continue to be impossible for teachers to police the use of generative AI. There is no reliable technology for detecting text produced by large language models.

The biggest tell of a ChatGPT-produced essay is that it is often *too fluent*, without the inevitable syntactical hiccups that come coupled with human-produced text. But how are we going to police and punish students for turning in work that is "better" (on this surface-level criteria) than what we believe they're capable of doing?

SORRY, KID, YOU'RE NOT THIS SMART

It is hard to pinpoint the inciting incident that led to the status quo, a bad status quo, regarding the state of writing in American schools.

In a previous book, *Why They Can't Write: Killing the Five-Paragraph Essay and Other Necessities*, I traced the origin point to *A Nation at Risk*, a report ginned up by a commission established by Ronald Reagan's Department of Education that warned of a society "presently being eroded by a rising tide of mediocrity that threatens our very future as a Nation and people."

This established the narrative of failing schools, and what schools were failing at was preparing future generations to fight off the rising economic and technological might of foreign powers. While *A Nation at Risk* was published in 1983 in the midst of the Cold War with the Soviet Union, the commission's chief concern at the time was Japan, which seemed to be ahead in terms of technological innovation.

Those Sony Walkmans I and every other kid were walking around with weren't manufactured in Detroit.

The report established an ethos suggesting the underlying purpose of an education is to secure material advantage in the competition against others, be they individuals in the marketplace or foreign nations on the world's stage. The dominant purpose of school would be to rank and sort students against standards and one another. These rankings would be used to determine not only which students were worthy but which schools and teachers were operating effectively as well. This competition would make sure the best and brightest were rising to the top while also, in theory, lifting the boats of the less capable.

Initiatives such as George W. Bush's No Child Left Behind and Barack Obama's Race to the Top were predicated on the same worldview. Education is a journey toward a single destination called *proficiency*, measured according to tests that must be standardized so we can properly compare students, schools, and teachers against one another.

In theory, it all makes perfect sense. Figure out what is important for people to know and then measure how they're doing on knowing that stuff. In practice, it has been a disaster that has led to now multiple generations of students becoming increasingly disengaged from school while failing to deliver improved performance even on the dubious metrics of these standardized tests.

What happened is an example of Campbell's law, named for Don Campbell, a sociologist who studied evaluation, including evaluation in schools, and declared, "The more any quantitative indicator is used for social decision-making, the more apt it will be to distort and corrupt the social processes it is intended to monitor."

In other words, when a measurement is a genuine indicator of underlying conditions and activities, it is a useful benchmark for progress. When stakes are attached to the benchmarks themselves, the corruption of the underlying practices is almost inevitable.

Campbell's law manifests itself in schools through the use and abuse of standardized tests, where the scores on those tests come to stand in for learning, no matter what methods have been deployed in the service of raising those scores. Rather than being a tool to gauge students' cognitive abilities, tests have become an exercise in seeing how well you do on the test.

This results in writing instruction that encourages students to work with templates—like the five-paragraph essay—while writing according to prescriptive rules (never use *I*, put the thesis at the bottom of the first paragraph, etc.) that are easily scored against a standardized scale but which have little to no relationship with the kinds of experiences that reflect a genuine engagement with the challenge of writing inside a rhetorical situation, something I first learned in Mrs. Goldman's class when she made me write those instructions for a PB&J sandwich.

I witnessed this devolution firsthand over the course of my career as fewer students arrived having had authentic writing experiences as part of their schooling. Smart, curious, college-ready students saw writing not as an opportunity to think and learn but as a box-checking exercise meant to demonstrate proficiency. B. F. Skinner's teaching machine may have failed, but students have been incentivized to behave and write like an algorithm in order to please the measurements by which they're judged.

Students using ChatGPT to complete assignments that don't mean anything to them and seem unconnected to learning is only sensible. This is not a character defect of students but the sign of a bad disconnect between schooling and learning.

This disconnect has largely and unfortunately been normalized as an inevitable by-product of producing work for the purposes of being evaluated by a teacher in a system designed around ranking and sorting rather than fostering learning.

Seeing the capabilities of ChatGPT, Michael W. Clune, an English professor at Case Western Reserve University, observed that the application generated "essays that meet all of the official criteria for student writing: They have a thesis; they are polished, coherent, and well-argued; they support their points with evidence. They also lack any trace of surprise or originality, make no new connections, and are devoid of any striking use of language or evidence of individual human sensibility."[1]

That does not sound like a description of good writing, and yet according to Clune, these ChatGPT efforts would also receive a better-than-passing grade in his course because of their syntactical fluency. Considering this, Clune has come to believe that what he'd been asking his students to write was, in his words, "bullshit." Now, in ChatGPT, we have an application that can produce "bullshit" on demand. This suggests to me that the "official criteria" Professor Clune was using is not particularly meaningful.

Though, that his students were producing bullshit was not news to Clune made apparent only with the arrival of ChatGPT. Just a couple of years into his career, he realized that grading student work made him "die a little," and he "concluded that such papers have no conceivable educational or intellectual value—for myself, the student, the college, or the world." Clune had spent eighteen years on the job, believing that what he was asking students to do had no value, but it is ChatGPT that forced him to confront this fact for the first time in concrete ways.

Clune seems to understand that he has been allowing academic cosplay to pass for the real thing, to allow BS to pass for substantive thinking, and yet by his own reckoning, he's been engaged in this dynamic that serially causes him to "die a little" for the bulk of his career. His feelings may not be universal, but they are extremely common.

I have witnessed dozens of professors offer sentiments similar to Clune's during my career teaching writing.

Professors are not the only ones who view the writing done in college this way. Writing in *Harvard Magazine* in March 2024, Harvard undergraduate Aden Barton lamented the purely "transactional" nature of writing in college, producing work for the purpose of earning a grade, but no more.

> I've noticed that I often internalize readings or assignments only insofar as they help me to succeed in a class, leaving no time to genuinely ruminate on the material.

> I've often had to pause to ask myself, "Do I agree with what I'm writing?" Mostly, though, I forgot even to ask that question: I've become so focused on crafting a palatable essay that the content almost becomes irrelevant.[2]

Here, then, is an example of what I mean when I call ChatGPT not a threat but an opportunity. No one—not professors, not students, not employers—believes the status quo is serving us well. The fact that ChatGPT can produce work that passes muster against the criteria that has come to matter in college courses should be a warning sign about the very work we are doing.

I don't want to come across as holier-than-thou. I incentivized the production of bullshit by students for many years. I engaged in a highly prescriptive teaching process that had students jumping through hoops with me coaching them every step along the way in an effort to get them to write something for which I could give a good grade. And yes, I too died a little while I was grading.

Why and how did we get to the point where students are producing bullshit and instructors are dying (a little)?

If we're going to confront what ChatGPT means for the kind of reading and writing students should be doing in school, we have to get down to the root values of what is important and meaningful about the writing we ask students to do. My experience teaching first-year college writing led me to believe that we weren't giving students the experiences they needed long prior to the arrival of ChatGPT. If anything, ChatGPT is the kick in the ass we need to rethink our approaches.

ChatGPT is not threatening anything meaningful, because it is not capable of producing any output that conveys meaning. If we want students to produce meaningful work, let's go ahead and do that.

There are three principles that can help us think about how to make ChatGPT largely irrelevant to the work we ask students to do and make choosing to outsource work to it a less attractive proposition for students.

1. Foster engagement through appreciation.
2. Build rigor through authentic challenge.
3. Make learning visible through reflection.

FOSTERING ENGAGEMENT THROUGH APPRECIATION

The evidence that school is largely an alienating experience for students is rather overwhelming. Pre-pandemic research from Gallup shows that a student's level of engagement with school declines every year after fifth grade, until ultimately, by eleventh grade, a majority of students are either "not engaged" or "actively disengaged."[3]

As far back as 2013, an American Psychological Association study found that over four in five students found school very stressful.[4] In 2018, a survey from the American College Health Association revealed that two-thirds of students "felt overwhelming anxiety" in the preceding twelve months.[5]

A 2022 study by Tyler Black, an emergency pediatric psychiatrist and researcher in adolescent psychiatry, was able to show that greater incidences of pediatric suicides and pediatric mental health emergency room visits are correlated with school being in session.[6] While it is broadly held that the pandemic years were damaging to the mental health of young people, pediatric suicides decreased significantly during that period, as students were relieved of many of the stresses of schooling.[7]

These issues have only been exacerbated by the pandemic and post-pandemic conditions. Chronic absenteeism is at an all-time high, and student anxiety and depression continue to climb. It is indisputable that schools are failing to give students the kinds of experiences that allow them to develop capacities that will serve them well going forward, leaving them stressed out and seeing little purpose in school, other than as a route to a credential.

We're now on at least our second or third generation of students who experience school not as an opportunity for learning but as a grim march through proficiencies, attached to extremely high stakes, stakes often measured by tests that are not reflective of genuine learning. An LLM-enhanced school experience does nothing to address these issues and in fact would have the opposite effect, putting each student on an individual track running parallel to the tracks of other students without ever intersecting.

Dan Meyer, the math educator who works for Amplify and sees alienation and disbelonging as the key challenges inside of schools, believes that students enter school armed with a desire to answer two core questions: (1) "Who am I?" and (2) "How do I do this?"[8]

"Who am I?" is a question of identity formation and is multifaceted, as students try to understand themselves in relation to other individuals, to the world, and to forces like systems of power. "How do I do this?" is concerned with the nuts and bolts of academic subjects, but as Meyer observes, it also invokes deeper questions about the self, with emphasis on the *I* rather than *this*.

There is both significant satisfaction and great power in developing and recognizing one's own capacities, as happened to me (far too late) when I worked at Leo J. Shapiro and Associates after graduate school. We should instill this knowledge in students much earlier, and to do that, they must first be engaged. A good way of getting students engaged is to stoke their appreciation for the inherently interesting parts of learning a subject.

In fact, I believe every course should start with appreciation.

Back in high school, I signed up for a course in music appreciation taught by the assistant band director because everyone said it was easy.

Class primarily consisted of listening to music while watching the assistant band director stare wistfully into the distance as he tapped his foot in time or mimed the fingering of an imaginary brass instrument. We listened to music, and we *appreciated* it by talking about what we'd heard—no wrong answers, just observations. We did some classical and some popular music (like the Beatles), but the assistant band director was a jazz head, so we got lots of jazz, a genre my father listened to, but which I'd been steadfastly against, possibly for that reason.

At first, the class was almost painfully awkward. We would listen, the assistant band director would smile at us, ask what we heard, and we stared back at him, nearly silent.

Uhh . . . a saxophone?

We had nothing to say. What had we heard? Uhh . . . music . . . we guess?

But he modeled responses for us, pointing out particular phrasings or how instruments might interact inside a piece. Maybe a little overarching theory was sprinkled in, but I don't really remember any specifics. I do remember after listening to Dave Brubeck's "Take Five" and having the assistant band director tap out the time signature on the desk, experiencing a literal moment of appreciation—the roiling sense of movement, its peculiar swing driven by the 5/4 beat. He played the song again, and we tapped along. I didn't know my fingers could do that.

Later in the semester, the assistant band director played Brubeck's "Blue Rondo à la Turk" and while it was playing asked us about the time signature. Someone blurted out 5/4, like you'd do if you were recalling something from memorization for a quiz, but before the assistant band director could answer, someone else said, "No, it's 9/8." We tapped it out. He was right.

My personal epiphany was listening to a recording by the great guitarist Django Reinhardt and hearing the very faint sound of his fingers scraping against the guitar strings as he was playing. You had to listen closely because it was underneath the music, but that was the point: I realized I was listening closely, more closely than ever before.

The assistant band director knew we were all there because the course was an easy A, which in a way seemed to free him up to teach us something more meaningful, that the world will reveal itself to you if you learn to pay attention.

We learned that we possessed the powers to observe (listen to) the world and interpret that world for ourselves. I'm confident we made no discoveries not already known by many before us, but we were being taught to believe in ourselves as creators of knowledge, self-knowledge above all.

Hindsight and many years of teaching have allowed me to see what a gift this was, to be exposed to an approach that made space for students to practice their own values. If the goal was to appreciate music, the goal was met. We not only appreciated music, we appreciated our own abilities to appreciate music.

Sadly, students often seem to experience school as a steady beat of disempowerment, a demonstration of the ways they are found wanting, all the things they do not know. In contrast, showing the subjects we teach as being inherently fascinating—and more importantly, open to inquiry, which pays off in knowledge—is inherently empowering and motivating. Getting students to recognize that they do know things and that on the things they know they can build additional knowledge is an excellent route to increased engagement. It is at the core of what I ask students to do utilizing my framework of the writer's practice.

The good news is writing that values the process, and the practice-building aspects of these activities, rather than reducing them to limited proficiencies that fit on a standardized test, provides an experience which helps raise student self-knowledge, and self-efficacy when it comes to writing. Once students are engaged and empowered, we can increase the rigor of the work by requiring students to become self-regulating.

BUILDING RIGOR THROUGH AUTHENTIC CHALLENGE

After diagnosing the systemic and pedagogical problems that stand in the way of empowering students and teachers engaging in authentic, meaningful writing activities in *Why They Can't Write*, I decided to stand behind my own beliefs and produce a book of writing experiences that would address the deficiencies I'd perceived. Rather than putting them through pro forma school writing exercises, I wanted students to have to wrestle with the challenges writers face when writing for audiences in authentic rhetorical situations.

That book, *The Writer's Practice: Building Confidence in Your Nonfiction Writing*, is filled with writing experiences ranging from very standard academic artifacts, like argument summaries, to more elaborate exercises, like writing an alternate history, to forms you'll rarely find explored in schools, like topical jokes or rants.

The experiences were based in my many years of experimenting as part of my teaching practice, as it became clear to me the most important factor in terms of the quality of a student's output and the depth and breadth of their learning was how interested they were in the task at hand. I wanted my first-year writing students to become writing problem solvers, so I had to give them interesting problems to solve.

In order to achieve this, every experience starts with a question a student has to answer. For example, an experience that is meant to result in the student having written a review starts with "Should I . . . ?" as in "Should I go see that movie?"

Every experience also has an authentic audience and a suggested process that requires students to go through a multistep journey on the way to completion. By framing the experience as problem-solving rather than students thinking about writing to "standards" that are largely abstract, they must engage with the specific needs of their audience and the demands of the occasion. They are learning that every piece of writing is a custom job rather than something written to a template for a grade, and that no two writers will produce the same piece, even if they are working from similar material, like writing reviews of the same movie.

This often creates a certain amount of—what I believe is productive—uncertainty for students. By focusing students on the demands of the rhetorical situation, I'm increasing their responsibility. Rather than being able to ask me, the teacher/authority if they're doing the right thing, they must continuously reflect on whether or not they're meeting the demands of the occasion and solving the writing problem. Part of being empowered is embracing responsibility, and I do as much as possible to make students responsible for the impact of their writing.

The writing students produce through this kind of process is not necessarily better in terms of the quality of the product, but that product, rather than being something merely graded in terms of proficiency, instead becomes the evidence of a learning experience. This is where reflection comes in.

MAKING LEARNING VISIBLE THROUGH REFLECTION

Once students have completed the work, we have to assess what's happened using a method that communicates what's been achieved with the work in terms of the quality of problem-solving inside the rhetorical situation.

That's my job. I provide students with feedback that's designed to give them something to consider as they engage in their own reflection about the process they've gone through in completing the experience.

We're looking to understand what's been learned so the students can take ownership of and then build on that learning from experience to experience.

For that reflection, during the experience, I ask students to consider the following:

- What have you discovered that is new to you?
- What line, idea, or concept occurred to you while writing that you hadn't planned on?
- What are you confident in? What are you confused by?

These questions should be recognizable as my attempt to make the reality of writing as thinking visible to the students themselves. It is also a move to make students responsible for the amount of rigor they bring to work.

After the experience is complete and students have received the feedback and commentary from me, I ask them to reflect on some additional questions:

- What do you know now that you didn't before? (This is a question of both knowledge of subject matter and the writing process.)
- What did you do in completing this experience that you're going to do again in the future?
- What did you do in completing this experience that you think would be a bad idea to repeat?

The grade students receive is based only partially on the final written artifact they've produced during the experience and is in fact much more heavily weighted toward what they *learned* in the process of completing the experience. The writing is used as evidence of learning (or not learning, as the case may be) rather than the instrument by which students are ranked and sorted. Students must consistently consider their self-perceived progress on the questions of who they are and what they're learning.

This process and these reflection questions are not vulnerable to being outsourced to ChatGPT, because ChatGPT has no knowledge of the students' thoughts or access to what it was like to do the experience. More importantly, when students are asked to share their knowledge and insights with the world, and those insights are given value, they will turn away from the bullshit that Professor Clune (and I) detect coming from students.

I know this approach works because I lived it, seeing the difference it made in what students do in class.

I also know it works because students say so.

For several years, material from *The Writer's Practice* has been used in a summer enrichment project sponsored by the Daniel Murphy Scholarship Fund for rising eighth graders from the Chicago public schools. As part of the seminars in being successful high school students, the rising eighth graders did experiences from *The Writer's Practice* for sixty to ninety minutes a day.

At the end of the week, these students were asked the same thing I ask my students at the end of the semester: "Who are you (now) as a writer?"

Here are some things students said:

My attitudes toward writing have changed. I used to view writing as something stressful, but now I have learned steps to make it easier. My writing process has also altered. I used to just start writing, but now I have learned that prewriting plays a crucial role.

I honestly didn't think I would have as much fun writing this week, but the truth is, I loved it. [This week] brought out a writer inside me I didn't know was there in the first place. I have written for myself before, but when I was writing this week, I just didn't want to stop. I was an untamable beast. This past week truly showed me how fun and enjoyable writing can be.

My attitude toward writing has always been that I love it. I haven't enjoyed all of the writing I've been doing in my life, though. I did the same analytical essay for two years, seventh and eighth grade. After a while, it got repetitive. However, this week I feel like the prompts have given me the chance to put my opinion in my writing, which in turn made my experience more enjoyable. I've become more aware of the writing process that I have, and I even made a few changes to ensure that I am writing the best I can.

If we value engagement, if we value student agency, to me, these look like successes. I do not know how these experiences and attitudes would translate in terms of performance on a standardized test. To be honest, I don't care, but I'd argue an engaged student is more likely to perform well on a standardized test than a disengaged student.

I don't intend to suggest that I've unlocked some kind of secret sauce that magically gets students engaged with school and writing. Not every student suddenly springs to life when given these kinds of experiences. There is no universal solution to the challenge of getting students engaged, and teaching and learning are hard.

Unlike the featureless texts that ChatGPT churns out, human writing is spiky, weird, and messy. This is particularly true when we are in the midst of trying to figure stuff out through writing, which is always going to be the case with students. If I wanted my students to become confident writers, I had to let them write, and if I was going to let them write, I had to value something other than the ability to BS proficiently.

That's ChatGPT's job.

In the end, however, the most important value we need to embrace is that writing is *hard*. The drive to make it so students could prove their proficiency led to bleeding the most challenging and difficult-to-assess aspects of writing out of the process. Rather than reducing writing in schools to an essence, we drained it of substance.

Next, we have to consider the kind of reading we want students to do because without reading, there is no writing.

CHAPTER 13

Reading Like a Writer

I am cautious of perpetuating a perennial narrative about the shortcomings of students, that each generation is somehow deficient as compared to what came previously. The world changes, and we should change our perceptions with it. All that said, it seems clear that we have some challenges when it comes to young people and reading.

I'm not talking about the most recent round of reading wars centered on the so-called science of reading movement. I am a conscientious objector to this war, which has taken on a bizarre cultural-conflict flavor, where people genuinely interested in exploring how to best help students learn to read have been infiltrated by political forces who never miss a chance to undermine the public's faith toward public schools. When a group both champions the science of reading *and* banning books, it seems clear that they are not acting out of a passion for phonics.

When we talk about reading, it makes a big difference as to what we're talking about. The science of reading movement is focused almost exclusively on the decoding aspect of reading, the recognition of words on the page. This makes sense because decoding is a necessary precursor to other aspects of reading.

As necessary as decoding is, by itself, it doesn't mean much when we think about the kind of reading we ultimately want students to be capable of: reading that gives students access to texts that they can make use of for their own intellectual purposes, reading that supports thinking and writing. This is the deep reading discussed in a previous chapter.

Having witnessed firsthand what happened to student attitudes toward writing as it was flattened by the demands of standardization, I fear a repeat trip into the land of Campbell's law when it comes to reading, as so much energy is poured into making sure students can decode and much less attention is paid to providing students the kinds of experiences that turn them into enthusiastic and well-rounded readers.

There are other reasons to worry beyond identifying a predictable pattern about to repeat.

In the words of education and social policy reporter Rachel Cohen, what's already happened in the United Kingdom regarding reading instruction offers a "cautionary tale."[1]

Screening for phonics knowledge and explicit teaching of phonics became law across the UK in 2012. This law mandated "up to three years of daily hour-long phonics lessons." These lessons were focused on "synthetic phonics," the teaching of phonemes (essentially the sounds letters make) using books judged to be at the level of current student proficiency. Subsequent research showed that this extreme emphasis on students learning phonemes from texts designed to be decoded—rather than read for meaning or to be engaging and enjoyable—harmed students' overall development as readers. Rather than such an overwhelming focus on synthetic phonics, superior instruction required an integration of whole texts that also helped students build the skills of interpretation and comprehension.[2]

We already have many warning signs about a disconnect between students and the building of robust reading practices.

The percentage of students who "read for fun" every day or nearly every day in the US was halved between 2012 and 2023.[3] New curriculum adopted in New York City public schools to provide the intensive phonics instruction favored by science of reading advocates will have elementary age students reading zero whole books.[4]

Mark Seidenberg, a professor and neuroscientist whose research significantly informed the *Sold a Story* podcast that triggered a boom in attention about reading curriculum, believes we're already failing at implementation and overshooting the mark. He told Cohen, "There are big opportunity costs and the clock to fourth grade (an important milestone in reading development) is ticking. You only want to do a lot of instruction on these components enough to get off the ground."

These canned curriculums are extremely profitable for the educational publishers who provide them, but one-size-fits-all mandates ignore that different individuals learn to read differently. Yes, phonics are key for lots of readers, but not for *every* reader. Some students arrive in school already having surpassed what basic phonics instruction can do for them, while others need to build knowledge from scratch.

Those of us working in college classrooms have noticed changes in student attitudes and approaches toward reading. Over the years, out of necessity, I started to explicitly teach students the kind of reading they were expected to do in class. Students were skilled at pulling out subject matter and information like you'd be quizzed on for reading comprehension, but much less practiced at analysis and interpretation.

Writing in February 2024, Adam Kotsko, a longtime professor at a liberal arts college, remarked that after routinely assigning around thirty pages of reading for a class period, "students are intimidated by anything over 10 pages and seem to walk away from readings of as little as 20 pages with no real understanding. Even smart and motivated students struggle to do more with written texts than extract decontextualized takeaways. Considerable class time is taken up simply establishing what happened in a story or the basic steps of an argument—skills I used to be able to take for granted."[5]

Again, this is not about defective students. Students are the products of what they've been rewarded for doing inside the system. By treating reading and writing as isolated skills, rather than as whole practices that exist in a dynamic world, we've allowed academic cosplay to substitute for learning. By treating students like standardized products, we've lost sight of the complexities and rigor that must attach to learning.

The top-down initiatives that have been visited on teachers and classrooms traceable to *A Nation at Risk* sidestep that the work of teaching is the work of *differentiation*, and by claiming that there is a hard and fast "science" to reading loses sight of the much more complicated cultural and social dynamics around all the things we're talking about when we say that someone can "read."

We don't only need to teach children to read, we need to *make* readers. I understand that this may seem like some kind of special pleading from a writer and writing teacher, but the ability to take in, understand, and synthesize information is a foundational, uniquely human skill that separates us from large language models.

The good news is that this is a process that is embedded in our cognition. When working with students, I describe it using the acronym ROAS, which stands for: react, observe, analyze, synthesize.

ROAS is built on the fact that we are constant "readers" of the world around us, taking in information and drawing conclusions from it. When I was teaching at Clemson University, in order to illustrate our native abilities at observation and inference, I would describe particular modes of dress and ask students what they thought they knew about that person. If I said, "Collared pastel shirt, khakis, boat shoes, and Croakies sunglasses holder around the neck," the students would say, "Frat guy." This included the students in a fraternity. (We would also talk about the dangers of stereotyping.) My goal was to show that students could quickly translate their human perceptive abilities to reading and interpreting texts.

One assignment I would give for students to practice this process asks them to answer the question, "What's so funny?" This question and the process I provide them is designed to result in the students producing a rhetorical analysis of a work of humor, but if I just told students to write a rhetorical analysis of a work of humor, the vast majority of them would have no idea as to what I'm asking them to do. The average reader might not either, and yet it's something anyone can do through a process of reacting, observing, analyzing, and synthesizing.

The goal of a rhetorical analysis of a work of humor is to explain why something is funny not in the mechanical sense but in the way it utilizes an audience's beliefs about the world to trigger a humorous response. Laughter is an involuntary reflex, but when triggered by a joke, that reflex is built upon a foundation of experience, values, and cultural knowledge. When we laugh, it is an acknowledgment that some commentary has hit a target, a "truth" revealed. With the experience, I'm asking students to uncover one of these truths by paying close, sustained attention to a text.

The first step of the process is for the students to literally react, to laugh at whatever they find funny and make a note of what was happening as they laughed. In class, we will have spent a lot of time prior to this exposing ourselves to things we find funny, ranging from the crudest physical "comedy" as found on bloopers shows like *America's Funniest Home Videos* or *Tosh.0*, to classic satire like Jonathan Swift's *A Modest Proposal.* We have been practicing noticing our reactions and honoring those noticings as something worth thinking about.

I then turn them loose on a piece of comedy of their own choosing. I ask them to react, to literally record where they laugh, and then go investigate that laugh's origins.

One example I've used is a joke delivered by Tina Fey as cohost (with Amy Poehler) of the Golden Globe Awards.

> *George Clooney married Amal Alamuddin this year.*
>
> *Amal is a human rights lawyer who worked on the Enron case, was an advisor to Kofi Annan regarding Syria, and was selected to a three-person UN commission investigating rules of war violations in the Gaza Strip.*
>
> *So tonight, her husband is getting a lifetime achievement award.*

When I first heard this joke live on television, I recall a barking "Ha!" of recognition coming out of me. As jokes go, it is pretty standard stuff, a well-executed setup and punch line, but no more than that. But it triggers this reaction, kicking off our ROAS sequence.

Next, I ask students to observe the world surrounding the joke. In the case of the Tina Fey gag, we might note that this is a fancy Hollywood event with famous and beautiful people gathered together to celebrate the year's best TV and film entertainment. One of the staples of the Golden Globes broadcasts is the candid shots of celebrities hobnobbing with one another, shown as the broadcast cuts to commercial.

We might observe that in Fey's description of (now) Amal Clooney's work, she has listed three historically bad world events. I can't help but note that two of them are still ongoing almost ten years since Fey delivered the joke.

We might note that Amal Alamuddin does indeed now go by Amal Clooney, and as accomplished as she clearly was and is, she is also noted for her great beauty, and going forward, whatever she does on her own, she will be first known as the wife of a world-famous actor—an inherently sexist notion that nonetheless often passes without comment.

Next, we can turn toward analysis, gathering our observations into ideas and claims around the nature of celebrity and how celebrity obliterates other qualities. In the case of Amal Alamuddin, she becomes, in the words of Linda Holmes, author and NPR podcaster, "a red carpet accessory"[6] as opposed to the influential human rights activist and attorney with her own list of impressive accomplishments.

The directions students may take their own thoughts once they have laid bare the underlying dynamics of Fey's joke are infinite. I have had students pivot to writing about the power of social media and the way it reduces three-dimensional individuals into (literal) images and how this is a particular problem for women. I have had others argue that celebrity is itself a worthy and significant achievement, a "power multiplier" in one student's words, that benefits Amal Clooney's work, so we shouldn't be so quick to assume this is a kind of attention she does not want. It is sometimes thrilling to see where the minds of these people that have been shaped by very different experiences from my own go.

Of course, some students struggle with this experience. They sometimes think it's weird or silly to go looking underneath the surface of a text. If it makes you laugh, they think, who cares why or what it means?

But if and when they get past this initial skepticism, students will experience firsthand what it is to think through writing. They will join the academic conversation, adding knowledge to the world. If this is not the goal of postsecondary education, what is?

This experience translates directly to a form of reading that can become a kind of superpower, the reading skill that allowed me to succeed when Leo Shapiro told me to write that questionnaire for the environmental nonprofit. That skill is reading like a writer.

Back when I was describing what it means to have a writing practice and I compared a writer's practice to a chef's practice, I said that one of the essential parts of a chef's practice is to be able to taste a dish and then remake that dish by breaking it down into its component parts.

Reading like a writer is doing the same thing, only with a piece of writing. Having experienced a piece of writing, the writer then seeks to understand the components that make the whole, to get under the hood and examine the way the parts of the engine work together to make the car go zoom. Reading like a writer requires a deep practice of critical thinking and is something students should spend far more time on than learning content in school because it allows them to become true experts at thinking, which then significantly speeds later content acquisition. Rather than new information being stacked randomly inside our personal memory palaces, think of reading like a writer as a way to give the information you already have an external wrapping of Velcro, making it much easier for the new stuff to adhere.

One of the ways I try to get students reading both closely and deeply is to sensitize them to the impact of seemingly very small choices on how audiences respond to a text. In order to convey how these nuances work, I employ an experience called "Right Word, Almost Right Word," an homage to a Mark Twain dictum that "the difference between the right word and the almost right word is the difference between lightning and the lightning bug."

I first ask students to unpack the metaphor, and they quickly grasp that Twain is talking about a significant gap in impact between a wee green glow from a lightning bug and the sudden shock of total illumination from a bolt of lightning. Next, I read a short passage from a text out loud, asking them to identify (react and observe) where they experience a jolt of lightning.

(Over the years, I've discovered that reading short texts out loud while asking students to attend to a specific response significantly ups their focus and concentration.)

One text I've often used is an essay by David Foster Wallace documenting his time on a cruise, "A Supposedly Fun Thing I'll Never Do Again," part of a collection of essays with the same title. I read this passage out loud:

> I have seen sucrose beaches and water a very bright blue. I have seen an all-red leisure suit with flared lapels. I have smelled what suntan lotion smells like spread over 21000 pounds of hot flesh. I have been addressed as "Mon" in three different nations. I have watched 500 upscale Americans dance the Electric Slide. I have seen sunsets that look computer-enhanced and a tropical moon

> that looked more like a sort of obscenely large and dangling lemon than like the good old stony U.S. moon I'm used to.[7]

Students flag a number of different moments, "sucrose beaches" or the moon like an "obscenely large and dangling lemon," but by far, the most noted passage is this one: "I have smelled what suntan lotion smells like spread over 21000 pounds of hot flesh."

As I read the passage out loud, I glance up and see some noses wrinkle in disgust. After they've identified it as worthy of further consideration, I will read the passage several more times in varying cadences with different emphasis on different words, "I have smelled what suntan lotion SMELLS LIKE spread over 21000 pounds of HOT FLESH." Each time I read it, students recoil, the language losing zero potency with repetition. In fact, it's the opposite.

I ask them what's going on.

"Flesh!" they cry. "It's so gross!" We talk about the diminished impact of a slight substitution, the almost-right word moving into place: "I have smelled what suntan lotion smells like spread over 21000 pounds of hot *skin*."

"Skin isn't as gross," the students assure me, and they are correct. Say the word out loud, *flesh*. Consider the connotations of the word, *flesh*. Zombies feast on flesh. Flesh is . . . well . . . fleshy.

I ask students why Wallace would make this choice. Mind you, this is the second paragraph in an essay they have not read. They do not know anything about the full context of the piece, which is essentially a takedown of the American consumerist mentality of excess as manifested on a Caribbean cruise, as well as a meditation from Wallace's point of view in which he is troubled by how he is intermittently seduced by it. By the end, Wallace is disgusted with both himself and everyone else.

Some student will hit the nail on the head, something like, "It's about excess. Sitting around tanning, eating, partying is supposed to be fun, but he's saying it's too much."

After this, they may link that sense of excess to Wallace's use of repetition, starting each sentence with "I have," or "I have *smelled* what suntan lotion *smells like*," noticing that Wallace wants to sort of rub it in (pun intended), to make sure we cannot miss the moment. Sometimes students paying particularly close attention will recognize that the actual smell of the suntan lotion on the hot flesh is not specified, and yet every reader seems to have a strong sense of that smell.

That's a pretty amazing thing to notice when—as is often the case for many of my students—you've never been asked to look at writing in quite this way before. What this tells me is that reading like a writer even at an extremely close level of nuance is an ability most people possess provided they are given the opportunity to practice it. Over a forty-minute chunk of class, we will not move on from this passage as I ask students to look more closely, then look again to see what else they can see. I am asking them to read like writers, and in doing so, the entire world of the essay opens to them.

The rest of the world is open to them as well as they recognize they too can observe, to draw inferences from those observations and then conclusions from the collection of those inferences. This is thinking. This is discovering new knowledge, a decoder ring for the culture we live within.

In truth, what they are seeing and what students are experiencing is being awake and alive, and once you realize that you are awake, you can start to make some sense of the world.

Making sense of the world is the work of writing, but what happens when writing is buried under an avalanche of AI-generated "content"?

CHAPTER 14

Content vs. Writing

The biggest shift over the course of my life as a writer has been the transformation of writing into something known as "content."

Content is anything that can be consumed by an audience via a platform. Content is stuff where the primary purpose is to draw an audience to feed them advertising. Lots of content on the internet is writing, but there is also content made of words that does not qualify as writing. The meaning, purpose, and quality of the content is immaterial, provided it can be monetized through clicks.

There is no genuine communicative intent behind content.

With writing, there *is* a core intention to communicate and connect with others. This writing may be monetized through advertising or subscriptions or other means, but this monetization—while necessary to provide an outlet for the writing—is secondary to the writing itself. The *New York Times* has millions of subscribers and sells lots of ads, but the purpose of the paper is to provide news, information, analysis, and, okay . . . *Wordle* to an interested audience. All those routes for generating revenue are in service of that mission. This does not make the *Times* or other publications noble and pure, but at least for now, the goal of writing to communicate with an audience is at the core of the enterprise even if some of what they publish could be classified as mere content.

One of the most immediate and potentially damaging consequences of generative AI is its potential to drown us in content whose only purpose is to capture clicks to generate revenue through online advertising.

If this sounds like your current experience of the internet, get ready for it to become significantly worse.

HERE COMES THE FLOOD

Google search has been continuously degraded by the flood of content. At one point, Google genuinely worked as a tool to find the web-based information most relevant to your searches. But since Google makes most of its revenue through advertising, the top of those search results has become increasingly precious real estate. Popping up first if someone does a relatively generic search like "Chicago hotels" may pay significant dividends, as few people are going to get beyond the first page of results before clicking on a link.

Beneath this paid placement, however, lurks the world of search engine optimization (SEO), the manipulation of how content is categorized and ranked by search engines so as to lift that content to the top of a particular search string. In theory, SEO could work in the service of delivering the most relevant, highest-quality results that meet the needs of the person doing the search. In reality, SEO works, in the words of Amanda Chicago Lewis, writing at the Verge, "more like the Wizard of Oz projecting his voice to magnify his authority. The goal is to tell the algorithm whatever it needs to hear for a site to appear as high up as possible in search results, leveraging Google's supposed objectivity to lure people in and then, usually, show them some kind of advertising."[1]

Maximizing SEO has become a big business, the route toward which a website can gather eyeballs to which *they* can expose advertising. For a while, these websites were derided as clickbait, but at this point, just about the entire internet has become clickbait, much of it algorithmically generated, even prior to ChatGPT's release.

Perhaps I am revealing something about my character that I first noticed the depths of badness of this phenomenon by searching for information on celebrity net worth. Sometimes a guy gets curious about whether or not former *Saved by the Bell* costar Mario Lopez has managed to sock away enough dough to live a comfortable life.

Searching "Mario Lopez net worth" on Google brings up multiple pages on which you're primarily bombarded with ads, but in between those ads, you can make out some data algorithmically scraped from the internet and filled into a template to learn about Mario Lopez's salary (as host of *Access Hollywood*), his marital status, his tattoos, and his house in Glendale, California, valued at $1.9 million.

What I'd been fed by my search was a raft of digital flotsam washed up into a spot where people with too much time on their hands (me) might find themselves. Once captured, perhaps they are enticed by another link promising "shocking" photos of celebrities without makeup or a 40 percent discount on a novelty T-shirt imprinted with IF YOU'RE CLOSE ENOUGH TO READ THIS YOU'RE STANDING ON MY JOHNSON because who doesn't want to walk around wearing a T-shirt that would engender eye rolls from everyone save eleven-year-old boys?

It is impossible to quantify the proportion of junk to genuinely useful information on the internet, but surely the crap predominates, or at least seems to because it has been search engine optimized. The ways that generative AI will deliver an even greater wave of crap have already been revealed.

HIDING CONTENT BEHIND FAKE HUMANS

In November of 2023, on the platform formerly known as Twitter, someone named Jake Ward, self-identified as the founder of three different SEO-related companies, outlined the method by which he "pulled off an SEO heist that stole 3.6M total traffic from a competitor by using generative AI."[2] After extracting all the competitor's article titles, they used generative AI to create 1,800 new articles with the exact same titles, creating a kind of digital doppelgänger that they can boost above the original on search using superior SEO strategies.

Imagine this sort of activity carried off at scale, where every original piece with useful information has an inferior AI copy, a kind of endless doubling (or tripling or quadrupling) of content, all in the pursuit of clicks and advertising monetization. With generative AI, this could be carried off in close to real time as a popular or newsworthy piece is duplicated with the purpose of soaking up some measure of the traffic meant for the original. Over time, it becomes impossible to find the original among the copies. Given the propensity for generative AI to hallucinate false information, it could even become impossible to discern what's accurate and true in the midst of the digital cacophony.

Reflecting on the potential harm of this flood of AI-generated content, Ethan Mollick of the Wharton School of Business—and an early pioneer of employing generative AI tools as boosts to human productivity—remarked, "One side effect from AI is that the corpus of human knowledge from mid-2023 on will have to be treated fundamentally differently than prior to 2023. A huge amount of what you learned or think you know about how to evaluate images or text is no longer valid. Not an exaggeration."[3]

Ironically, the very information that's used to target users with advertising can no longer be reliably discerned from the output of generative AI. We could be looking at a world where algorithms meant to do sentiment analysis and glean consumer interest are working from text generated by other algorithms. Those algorithms will then generate more content to draw audience that is instead primarily "read" by other AI in an endless generative AI ouroboros. The nuttier thing is that some people will make a lot of money on this, at least for a while.

Whether or not audiences know and expect that a particular piece of writing is attached to a human exercising personal autonomy and agency has significant implications for how we use and assess that information.

Maybe this is why some early forays into AI-generated content have gone to great lengths to hide the role of AI.

There was a time where writing for *Sports Illustrated* would have been a dream come true for most journalists. Publishing continuously since 1954, the magazine became iconic and in the days prior to cable television and ESPN was essentially the chief conduit of national sports coverage. Its famous staffers included sports writing legends like Dan Jenkins, Frank Deford, George Plimpton, and Paul Zimmerman.

New issues came to our house on Thursdays, and I'd have to be sure to read it prior to my dad coming home from work and calling out, "Where's my *SI*?" practically the moment he walked in the door. The magazine would stay on his nightstand until the next issue arrived. I would beg my mom to temporarily unsubscribe and then resubscribe so we were eligible for the free *Sports Illustrated* football phone, a plastic piece of junk that I nonetheless deeply coveted.

The *Sports Illustrated* of late 2023 was much diminished, suffering years of declining circulation as the internet swallowed print, ultimately being sold off by Time Inc. to a private equity group, which in turn sold the license to publish *Sports Illustrated*–branded content to the Arena Group, a digital outfit that operates legacy publishing brands as quasi click farms.

Still, it might have been something of a thrill for Drew Ortiz to contribute to *Sports Illustrated*. Ortiz was not covering the big subjects, mind you, but everyone needs to get their foot in the door. In Ortiz's case, this took the form of writing about how you can "Play Like a Pro with the Best Full-Size Volleyballs."[4]

Drew is not a wordsmith, which perhaps explains why he was covering not even volleyball the sport but volleyballs the object, offering such choice insights as "Volleyball is one of the most popular sports in the world, and for good reason." And "Volleyball can be a little tricky to get into, especially without an actual ball to practice with." In Drew's bio at the *Sports Illustrated* website, it said he loved camping and hiking. A young white guy with brown hair, blue eyes, and a neatly trimmed beard looked out at the reader.

But as revealed by Maggie Harrison Dupré writing at Futurism, Drew Ortiz was a fabrication, his photo for sale at a website dedicated to generating AI headshots for nonexistent people. Ortiz is described as "neutral white young-adult male with short brown hair and blue eyes."[5] The human journalists at Futurism discovered a raft of nonexistent contributors fronting AI-generated content. When Futurism contacted the Arena Group, the fake bios and content disappeared.

Even more fakes were discovered at another Arena Group publication, TheStreet, originally founded by business television talking head Jim Cramer. At TheStreet, the fake bios included information and credentials meant to bolster the "author's" bona fides to dispense financial advice. The Arena Group responded by saying that the articles had come from a third-party contractor responsible for providing advertising content to their websites, saying Arena Group had no firsthand knowledge of how the content was produced.[6]

Sports Illustrated, perhaps once the most trusted brand in all of sports journalism, was washing their hands of responsibility for writing appearing under their banner because they could not be bothered to confirm that the garbage advertorials they were pumping out to scrape pennies from consumer attention were the product of genuine human thought and labor.

In a world where generative artificial intelligence allows for the mass production of misinformation and garbage and some companies are willing to hide the origin of this junk, how are we supposed to sort through the piles of content to know that we're dealing with something produced by actual, accountable human intelligences?

WELCOME TO "OBITUARY SPAM"

Thanksgiving weekend 2023, I experienced the damaging nature of the generative AI enshittified online universe firsthand. I woke up to the sad news delivered via social media that the writer Gabe Hudson had passed away suddenly over the holiday at the age of fifty-two. Hudson and I had been acquaintances for better than twenty years through our mutual association with the McSweeney's publishing outfit. Hudson had served as marine infantry in the first Gulf War and struggled with PTSD, experiences that he'd turned into his poignant and hilarious collection of short stories, *Dear Mr. President*.

Looking for news, I searched online and at the top of the results saw a handful of "obituaries" for Gabe. Clicking on these alleged obituaries, it became apparent that they'd been scraped from information on the internet and cobbled together using generative AI. The pieces included biographical information, extracts from reviews, and social media comments from friends mourning

Hudson's passing grafted into a clumsy recounting of Hudson's life filled with misinformation. Back on social media, I saw people linking to these articles, expressing sincere condolences, but also spreading digital crap all over the place, obscuring the truth of both Gabe Hudson's life and his tragic passing.

Gabe Hudson was a plenty successful writer, publishing work in the *New Yorker*, being named one of the best young novelists working by *Granta* in 2007, hosting a successful literary podcast, and being generally beloved by the relatively small community of which I suppose I must be a member, but he didn't rise to the level of fame that would garner him an obituary in the kind of outlet that conveys authority and could push the SEO'd, AI-generated refuse back into the sewer where it belonged. I grabbed my slingshot and took aim at the Goliath via a short remembrance at my Substack newsletter, which did me the good of allowing myself the cathartic pain of writing as feeling as I shared my perspective on the loss, but which did nothing to stop the garbage from continuing to accrue.

I began to despair about how far someone in the future would have to scroll to find something accurate about the life and death of Gabe Hudson.

McSweeney's cofounder Dave Eggers, feeling the same despair, emailed me, asking if he could add my remembrance to his and some others he was gathering at the McSweeney's website. He included an email address for others to send in their memories of Gabe—short or long, it didn't matter. Over just a few days, the contributions mounted, small, specific, indelibly human memories of Gabe Hudson the person, written by people who knew him.

This collaborative act of remembrance and celebration ultimately overwhelmed the bots, and if you search for an obituary for Gabe Hudson, the first or second link you will find is the page at the McSweeney's website.

Sadly, Gabe Hudson's passing is one example of what has come to be a much broader phenomenon driven by AI-generated content: obituary spam.

Writing at the Verge in February 2024, Mia Sato identifies numerous cases of literal misinformation about people's deaths rising to the top of Google search results thanks to gaming of the SEO metrics by companies specializing in AI content.[7]

The obituary spam takes advantage of "data voids" that, when there is a lack of information about a particular topic, single sources can rocket up the search rankings. Searching for a name plus the word *obituary* when that person is not a well-known public figure will dredge up the spam.

One hopes that a human writer working on an obituary would have at least some qualms about passing on misinformation about someone recently departed, but generative AI has no such capacity for thought or feeling. When death is the frontier of SEO optimization, you have to wonder if there's further to fall, but I've learned that there is no bottom.

NEW, FROM YOUR FAVORITE AUTHOR—NOT!

Another generative AI "innovation" that kicked in almost immediately is the theft of reputation of existing writers. Jane Friedman is a former editor who now works as a publishing consultant and educator, sharing resources and insights through her own website. In August of 2023, she noticed two new "books" had been linked to her author page at the public reviewing website Goodreads, which is owned by Amazon. By the titles (*Promote to Prosper: Strategies to Skyrocket Your eBook Sales on Amazon* and *How to Write and Publish an eBook Quickly and Make Money*), they were plausible offerings, except Jane Friedman had not written them.[8]

The books were for sale at Amazon, linked to Friedman's identity, and were quite possibly generated via an algorithmic scraping of her work. Friedman told CNN, "When I started looking at these books, looking at the opening pages, looking at the bio, it was just obvious to me that it had been mostly, if not entirely, AI-generated. . . . I have so much content available online for free, because I've been blogging forever, so it wouldn't be hard to get an AI to mimic me."[9]

In a cleverer attempt, an AI-generated book, *The Evolution of Jazz: A Century of Improvisation and Innovation* by Frank Gioia and Ted Alkyer, came into the world. The dual authors were designed to take advantage of the fact that Ted Gioia (*The History of Jazz*) and Frank Alkyer (publisher of *DownBeat* magazine) are two noted jazz experts. Conflating their names allows the scammers to avoid the direct charge of misappropriating a single author's identity while still making the book attractive to search engines.

Because both Gioia and Friedman have their own public platforms and were able to make a fuss, the scam was exposed and the books were pulled from sale, but in a world where generative AI reduces the cost of producing content to nearly zero and scammers can make a few bucks putting up bogus product before pulling and running, we can expect this to be a serial feature of the world going forward.

Seeing these various scams relying on generative AI for their execution, I begin to wonder, how is it going to be possible for writers to get paid to actually write?

Is there a space for writing amid all this content?

CHAPTER 15

On the Future of Writing for Money

Most of the time when I'm talking about writing in this book, I've been emphasizing writing as a process, an experience and activity where the experience itself is meaningful for both the writer and the audience for that writing. This value is intrinsic and eternal and has nothing to do with markets.

Writing is a tool by which we can experience and understand both ourselves and the world at large. I realize that there are people of different minds about this, but to me, that is the core purpose of education, and I've conducted my courses in accordance with those beliefs.

Abandoning these aspects of writing—something that's already happened to a significant extent prior to the arrival of large language models—would be (has been) a bad thing. But there's another aspect of writing that generative AI implicates, something that hits very close to home.

Writing is work. Writing is labor.

As I've experienced firsthand over my years as a writer, it is very strange labor and the truth is, there aren't all that many of us who are categorized as "writers." According to IRS data in 2022, there were 151,200 people employed as "writers and authors" in the United States. We are a relatively small group as compared to teachers (4 million), nurses (3 million), accountants (1.4 million), and lawyers (1.3 million).

We do outnumber marine biologists (about 4,800).[1]

Writing is strange because on the one hand, there is a very direct relationship between the labor and compensation. No writing, no money. However, the way that labor is compensated is often detached from the amount of work involved, and identical labor can be compensated in wildly different ways. Stephen King and I have both written novels. Only one of us is a millionaire.

For years, I wrote for free, producing work—mostly short stories—that was plenty time-consuming but which had no apparent value in the marketplace. I was operating under what I understood of the system at the time: try to publish a couple of things, get a book deal, land a professor job, and you've wound up in a relatively comfortable place doing things you like.

(That path didn't pan out for me.)

After a period of writing for free, where no one save my professors and classmates saw my writing, followed one where I wrote *and* published for free, or what back then we called *exposure*, an intangible benefit that sounded like an excuse for publications not to pay contributors. Ultimately, though, this did pave the way to writing for money, so maybe it was worth something after all. Gradually, and then suddenly, writing for exposure no longer made sense, and now I do very little if any writing that doesn't carry with it at least some promise of specific, tangible economic benefit. I do not write solely for the purpose of earning money, but if there weren't money attached, you probably wouldn't find me writing this book, given the opportunity costs connected with such an effort.

I spend a majority of my working hours every week writing, but the activity itself is not what's valued. No one pays me for the *hours* I spend tapping away at my computer or, more commonly, staring at the screen mining my thoughts for the language that will express what's in my head. I'm paid for the product that can then be monetized by my publishers. Every week for twelve or so years, I've delivered a six-hundred-word column to the *Chicago Tribune*, for which they pay me a fee. My editor does not ask me how long it took me to write those six hundred words and adjust my fee accordingly. Some weeks, this is no more than an hour or two of work, as the idea arrives with some flesh on its bones and the words come freely. Other weeks, that one column I turn in may stand in for two others that were completed in draft form but judged wanting by me.

As a writer, I am luckier than most to still have publishers that have agreed to pay regularly for my contributions given that publishing as a business has been in decline for a good chunk of my life. When I started writing my column for the *Chicago Tribune*, I was part of a twenty-four-page stand-alone books section (Printers Row), while now, many weeks I am the sole contributor of original books coverage in the Sunday paper. Newspaper and magazine journalists, be they print, digital, or some mix of the two, have been hit by a series of layoffs since the 2008 recession.[2] Digital publishing has provided brief respites from these declines, but more recently, large online players (Vox, BuzzFeed) have been laying off staffers as it becomes clear that revenue from advertising will not support sizable news-gathering and -writing organizations.

As fortunate as I feel, I would have still been luckier to have been working in the 1980s, when being a weekly columnist for a major metropolitan newspaper would've paid me a pretty handsome wage all by itself, with the potential for even more compensation via syndication.

Instead, I cobble together my living from a variety of sources, and according to the findings from a survey of writers conducted by the Authors Guild, I'm doing better than most. Of the over five thousand writers captured in the 2022 data, the median pretax income from their books was $2,000.[3] Even in a year when I don't publish a new book, I do at least a bit better than that thanks to royalties from a couple of earlier books that continue to sell a few thousand copies a year.

When you add in what's defined as "book-related" income (things like speeches or seminars), the median nudges up to $5,000 per year. For writers the Authors Guild categorizes as "established" (having published a book in 2018 or earlier), things are a little rosier, with the book-related median income coming in at a little over $23,000 per year.

By these metrics, with my solid middle-class income from writing and associated activities, I am crushing it, but unless and until this book takes the world by storm, I am well short of the top 10 percent of established authors who have median incomes of $275,000 a year. As a profession, writing is significantly top-heavy. "Established" writers, like me, can earn enough to keep rowing the oars toward the next destination. A relatively small handful of superstars qualify as high earners. Doing the math on the Authors Guild data suggests that there is a greater percentage of writers who are earning $250,000 a year than there are who make a sustainable middle-class living from their writing, with the overwhelming amount earning something like poverty wages from their writing alone.

I include this information not so anyone will feel sorry for the writers of the world. Most days, I feel truly fortunate to spend my time on this work. But it is important to recognize the structures of labor that underpin the work of writing because if the structures collapse—and there is already significant erosion pre–generative AI—something we claim to value will disappear and be unlikely to return.

Generative AI and the flood of content is a threat, but it is hardly the only one. The infrastructure that supports the labor of writing and writers has been eroding for a long time. Maybe forever. Maybe it never existed in the first place. Jane Austen died nearly broke at age forty-one in 1817. It's too bad she didn't live in a time when she could've spawned the "Austenverse," a real thing that reliably delivers Austen-derived works to a willing public today and keeps Jane Austen's writing present in the culture.

As Cathy Davidson argues in *Revolution and the Word: The Rise of the Novel in America*, well into the nineteenth century, there was no mechanism by which a writer could make it as a novelist in America. Davidson's book traces how the idea that being a novelist as a viable profession had to take conscious shape and then be bolstered by a comprehensive system of commerce, which allowed for novels to be distributed, bought, and read. For "novelist" to become a job, America needed to evolve both its culture *and* its economics. These were not natural forces at work.

We may be looking at similar needs because of generative AI if we want to preserve writing as part of our culture.

Mark Twain is perhaps the first, or at least the most famous, early example of an American writer who made a living from his writing, a living bolstered by barnstorming the country to present his work like an itinerant preacher or, more accurately, like a stand-up comic. By all accounts, Twain made lots of money from his writing that he then funneled into a series of late-nineteenth-century start-ups, including a typesetting machine that was supposed to be many times faster than existing technology in producing books. He also started his own publishing company, which launched well out of the gate with Twain's *Adventures of Huckleberry Finn* ("a modest success") and *Personal Memoirs of U. S. Grant*, which proved to be a big bestseller among Civil War veterans.[4]

But things went south, and by 1894, he'd declared bankruptcy, owing the equivalent of $2.4 million in today's dollars to various creditors, including authors.

His last big bet was on something called "Plasmon," a protein powder that Twain claimed could "end the famine in India."

By the first quarter of the twentieth century, the publishing houses whose names still grace the spines of what we read (Knopf,

Holt, Harper) had arisen out of the early, post–Industrial Revolution printing and publishing network, and there was an infrastructure in place to support the work of writers and novelists. This (along with some inherited wealth) is what allowed for Gertrude Stein's Paris salon of expats—including Ernest Hemingway, Sinclair Lewis, Sherwood Anderson, and F. Scott Fitzgerald—to hang out, think, and speak big thoughts (and pickle their livers) in between writing and publishing books.

During the Depression, the Federal Writers' Project stepped in to help keep writers—including Ralph Ellison, Nelson Algren, and Richard Wright—afloat.

Add in the array of periodicals, such as the *Saturday Evening Post, Esquire, Vanity Fair* that came to be known as the "slicks," which published short fiction and essays for amounts that would rival what midlist writers receive as advances for entire books today, and you had a system that could support a fair number of people in the work of writing.

I have something of a unique window into this era through a family connection—my father's uncle, who, for a time, was very hot stuff on the American literary scene, but who today is largely forgotten, except by me.

His name was Allan Seager, and E. J. O'Brien, the original editor of what would become the *Best American Short Stories* annual (established in 1915, still publishing today), once told a radio interviewer that the four best short stories written by Americans were "The Undefeated" by Ernest Hemingway, "The Triumph of the Sea" by Sherwood Anderson, "Sherill" by Whit Burnett, and "This Town and Salamanca" by Allan Seager.

I have photocopies of some of Seager's personal papers that have been retained by the family, and they provide interesting insights into what it was like to be a writer in that era. Reading Seager's papers will disabuse anyone of the notion that even when support for writers was relatively robust, a life as a writer is all about time spent contemplating big ideas about art. There is some of that, but there are also notes about needing to crank something out for one of the slicks because the garage roof is leaking.

Over time, as radio and then television became the dominant mediums for information delivery and storytelling, those slicks faded in prominence and were no longer a reliable place to go for a quick payday to fix that leaky roof. Today, you'll find novelists looking to make a living working in film and television rather than being able to rely on the income from their books.

It is easy to romanticize a past that seems like it must've been better, but the struggle of writers to find a way to support their work has been a constant in American life.

Given that writers and writing have survived all previous threats, I'm actually somewhat bullish on the prospect of writers and writing to find a way to navigate through the flood of content both already here and likely to be exacerbated by the advent of generative AI.

In fact, some models that have both promise (and peril) have already been established.

In 2021, Brandon Sanderson, a best-selling author of science fiction and fantasy, announced on the Kickstarter platform that he was setting out to raise $1 million as a crowdfunding effort for four yet-to-be-written novels. By the time the campaign was over, Sanderson had raised over $41 million.[5] This represents over

185,000 backers paying a minimum of $40 (for e-book copies of all four books) up to $500 to receive the four books in digital, print, and audio format, plus a "themed swag box" sent out in the months in which a new book is not released.

Having 185,000 people who are willing to purchase every book you release will make you a very successful author, particularly if you write multiple books a year, as Sanderson does. In a traditional publishing paradigm, Sanderson would generate millions of dollars of income to himself, but nothing close to $41 million. Sanderson is an author who has not only readers but fans, and the intensity of that fandom and the emotional pull of being able to support their favorite artist directly has people willing to pay much more for the product than they would to a publisher.

This is one possible future for writers and writing in the ChatGPT world. Find your people, lock them down directly, give them the product they want, and tempt your superfans with extras.

As his own publisher, Sanderson needs to handle the production of the books and fulfillment of the orders—no small task, but relative to cost, and compared to the expense of the same activities at publishers, it is an efficient operation.

Unlike traditional publishing, which must sprinkle copies around the nation's bookstores, Sanderson knows exactly how many physical books he needs based on the number of backers. There is no marketing necessary, as all product has been presold. It is an amazing model if you have the fandom to sustain it. Sanderson is an outlier in terms of the massive size of his haul, but the crowdsourcing model is a viable route for sustaining the work of many artists because it allows the writer to capture the lion's share of the revenue generated by their product.

Newsletters, of which Substack is the most prominent platform, work in a similar way. Readers pledge direct support to writers through monthly or annual subscriptions, with a relatively small number of readers aggregating into relatively significant income. By way of comparison, I make about the same money on an annual basis from my free newsletter—paid subscriptions are voluntary—as I do from the column I write for the *Chicago Tribune*, even though the audience for the newsletter is something like one-hundredth the size of the column in the newspaper. As a writer, I appear to be worth about the same whether or not I am aggregated under the banner of a publication in a consumer marketplace or disaggregated as a solo artist running a patronage operation.

It's also pretty clear for someone in my circumstances that in terms of growth opportunities, going solo is a far better proposition than continuing to write for legacy media outlets.

Some newsletter writers have proven themselves *much* more valuable as disaggregated operators. The authors with the largest subscription bases make seven-figure incomes, far more than they ever would writing under the banner of even the most prestigious publications. Many others who were writing because they are compelled to write but don't consider it their primary way to make a living can achieve at least some level of income from their newsletters. As few as seventy-five paid subscribers translates to a few thousand dollars a year. This must feel like quite a boon when the alternative is no income. The anecdotal evidence of people on the platform suggests that the newsletter model is incentivizing the production of more writing than would otherwise be publicly available.

Other platforms like Wattpad, which caters to serialized stories, allows for a handful of "stars" to make money through readers paying to unlock content. Stories first serialized on Wattpad can jump to traditional publishing models once some audience and buzz has been established. *Icebreaker* by Hannah Grace, a work of hockey romance, was originally serialized on Wattpad before being acquired by Atria, an imprint of Simon & Schuster, after which it became a *New York Times* bestseller, moving over one million copies.

Thanks to digital technology, which makes production and distribution easier than ever, self-publishing also continues to grow, increasing from around 260,000 titles in 2014 to almost 2.3 million in 2021.[6]

The disaggregated patronage model removes the gatekeeping of publishing and allows more writers at least a shot at finding an audience. In some ways, you could see it as the best of times for writers, since no one stands in the way of you putting your work in the world and attempting to connect with your audience. Platforms like Wattpad and Substack take care of the infrastructure for distribution so writers don't also need to be their own tech experts. Still, aside from that digital infrastructure, you're on your own.

Personally, I'm grateful to have a newsletter that allows me to reap some financial benefit from an activity I enjoy doing, but we shouldn't mistake a patronage model that requires people to amass groups of fans and patrons to make their work financially viable as a problem-free or sustainable approach to getting paid for the labor of writing.

For one, there is still the not-small matter of attracting an audience. A significant proportion of my newsletter audience comes from my existing readership at the *Chicago Tribune*. I did not have to start from scratch. Along the way, the most effective way to increase my audience has been for a newsletter post to attract the attention of another writer with an existing fandom to champion my work. While disaggregation may look like freedom, without a mechanism to draw attention to yourself, one's writing becomes only a series of trees falling in the forest without anyone to hear them. The financial success of newsletter, crowdsourcing, or other patron-focused business models is directly proportional to the size of one's audience prior to arriving at the platform.

Brandon Sanderson can reap the rewards of a massive crowdfunding haul because he was already an established author in traditional publishing. Other writers, including literary writers like George Saunders and Margaret Atwood, have found immediate success on Substack because they arrived as well-known voices.

It is great work if you can get it, but becoming a brand as much as a writer comes with its own complications. When you are a brand, your readers become more like "consumers," and one of the things consumers expect from brands is consistency. For Saunders, this isn't a problem, as his brand of authentic wonder and fascination with writing and reading *is* the core of his work.

Brandon Sanderson's novels all exist inside a universe of his own design, a playground in which his fans accept and enjoy that he is the all-powerful storytelling deity.

But for others seeking to establish themselves in a disaggregated space, the need to feed the brand may transcend the work itself, leading to what is known as *audience capture*. Failing to live up to one's brand image could result in a sudden abandonment by one's audience, the same risk any product faces in the marketplace. Any changes the writer may wish to make to their approach or emphasis must be weighed against the strength of the audience's attachment to the brand. This will undoubtedly influence the writing that gets done by writers.

As one audience exhausts itself, a writer may have to pivot to find fresh sources of readership and revenue. Matt Taibbi was once a muckraking journalist with a penchant for attacking corporate greed from a leftist perspective, describing Goldman Sachs as "a great vampire squid wrapped around the face of humanity, relentlessly jamming its blood funnel into anything that smells like money." He has since pivoted to making his way as a handmaiden to the needs of the ultra-wealthy, serving as one of Elon Musk's chosen vessels to disseminate the "Twitter files" information and now making a very comfortable living at a very popular Substack attacking his perceived enemies. This fan service is perhaps the most straightforward way to make an imprint in the disaggregated market, but being captured by your audience comes with other costs.

The Substack platform is saturated with advice from newsletter authors on how to best "monetize" your writing, advice that tends to cluster around making sure to focus on a fairly narrow subject, writing consistently (multiple times a week), and making sure to give the audience what they want. The upshot is that the writer must be prepared to put themselves on a treadmill of constant production and audience service in order to realize income from their work. If they grow, they will likely have to act as a kind of mini-publisher, staffing up with help on editing, promotion, or customer service. Less time will be spent writing.

Again, speaking personally, these are the last things I want to think about when it comes to writing, so I choose not to think about them, but this choice comes with its own consequences. My aggressive indifference to chasing audience results in a smaller audience. The freedom I give myself to range in topics or opinions means I am constantly alienating some of the readers I've managed to garner over the years. If I irritate a handful of readers of the *Chicago Tribune* with my thoughts, no one cares. But at the newsletter, I consistently lose readers over something I've written, and because of the nature of the platform, they are more than willing to tell me so. When I aired some thoughts about the "science of reading" movement akin to what I discussed in the chapter on reading and writing, I was accused of not wanting dyslexic students to ever learn to read, a stance I promise I do not hold. I'd inadvertently stumbled into a culture war issue masked as a pedagogical debate, and this reader wanted to make sure I knew I'd chosen the wrong side and would be punished for it to the extent they were able.

Another time, I lost a subscriber for praising the *Jack Reacher* novels originated by Lee Child because, to the reader's mind, I was glorifying violence as a solution to conflict. I have even lost subscribers because I took a single week off while on vacation.

Please know, I do not begrudge these people their choices. I would not want to pay six dollars a month or fifty dollars a year directly to a person whose opinions I find irritating, wrong, or even damaging. But it illustrates the downside of the freedom of disaggregation in that ultimately, you *are* alone. On Substack or any other newsletter platform, you get a chance to sing for your supper, but you'd better not lose your voice or alter your tune too much, lest your revenue stream dries up. This is a very peculiar kind of freedom.

The Substack model also requires the writer to share a chunk of their revenue with the platform: approximately 21 percent per subscription goes to Substack and its transaction servicer, Stripe. The ease and convenience of using the platform justifies the charge, no doubt, but platforms are not eternal, nor are the terms under which the platform owners allow writers to operate. This has already happened at Substack. To lure established writers to the platform in 2021, Substack offered advances against future revenue and even health insurance to a handful of people. This allowed writers established at legacy publications to take a chance on ramping up their newsletter audiences. In some cases, it was an excellent bet. But after the initial year, these subsidies ended rather quickly, and Substack stopped offering advances. Substack is well established, but Friendster, Myspace, and Napster would like a word about the ephemeral nature of platforms, even ones that achieve massive scale.

All available information suggests that Substack is a money-losing enterprise, existing on venture capital money in order to keep operating. In 2022, against a stated valuation of $650 million on less than $10 million of annual revenue the previous year, Substack abandoned an attempt to raise an additional $75–$100 million of private money. As of early 2023, Substack says they have paid out more than $300 million cumulatively to writers. Doing some back-of-the-envelope math suggests that in 2022, Substack the company still had less than $20 million in annual revenue derived from their share of the author subscriptions.[7]

Through this lens, Substack begins to look like what Cory Doctorow calls a "bezzle," a term he uses in reference to Uber and its failure to turn into a profitable enterprise, even as it continues to reap private funding.[8] A bezzle is "the magic interval when a confidence trickster knows he has the money he has appropriated but the victim does not yet understand that he has lost it," and Doctorow believes that venture-funded businesses like Uber that rest on private money funding an unprofitable business until somehow, through some unstated magic, that unprofitable business becomes profitable can be viewed as bezzles. In the short term, it's a nice thing for writers that Substack appears to be funneling venture capitalist money to writers, but it is unlikely to be sustainable long term. At some point, if the private funding dries up, the only alternatives are to increase prices on the reading audience or carve out a larger share of the writer's take for Substack.

If you let your mind wander to the potential schemes involving generative AI that may attach to these activities, the possibilities are endless. Imagine a tool inside of Substack that analyzes your post for its potential to generate readers and subscription revenue, suggesting edits to juice up interest. Substack believes that their platform is a vehicle for expanding the audience for human-created writing, but it's just as possible they've created an aquarium for writers that continues to add new species without increasing the size of the aquarium or amount of water. Ultimately, it becomes a competition for the limited resources rather than a mechanism that, in the immortal malapropism of George W. Bush, "grows the pie higher."

Substack may provide writers with the freedom to avoid the encroachment of generative-AI on their work—unless of course they *want* to incorporate it—but as of yet, the disaggregated model for writers and writing doesn't appear any more sustainable as a route toward supporting the work of writing than what came before.

From the audience's point of view, a disaggregated universe of writers makes it harder to find the next new voice you're interested in hearing more from. The legacy publishing that spawned this initial generation of unbundled writers will only continue to grow weaker, giving it less potency. The imprimatur that having published a book conveys now will no longer matter as much as more writers go directly to a patronage model and make significantly more writing newsletters than they would publishing books.

This will shape the kind of writing that is published, disseminated, and read. While I have been working on this manuscript, I've also been maintaining my newsletter with weekly posts. The newsletter is the equivalent of a first pass at thinking through a topic, and indeed, many ideas in this book first appeared in some form in a column, newsletter, or a blog post at Inside Higher Ed (my other steady gig). But because writing is thinking, the book itself is a *very different* thing from those pieces. The book is deeper, more considered, more integrated. This book will have received editorial input from smart, expert people, professional copy editing and production. I read many newsletters every week and enjoy them, but they are not the same thing as a full-produced book.

There is one other model worth considering—the writing collective.

In 2020, a private media conglomerate looked at the traffic and audience for a website called Deadspin—primarily an outlet for irreverent takes on sports and culture—and saw an opportunity for more aggressive monetization. After purchasing the site, the new owners essentially substituted a content-first strategy for what had previously been an idiosyncratic collection of individual writers following their passions. The demands for ever-increasing traffic alienated staffers and readers alike as the original spirit of the publication was drained from the virtual pages.

Fed up with new management, a group of nineteen writers broke off and established a new publication, Defector, as an employee-owned collective.[9] At the time, there was a handful of Deadspin contributors who could have landed at other publications or become solo artists at a newsletter platform like Substack, but instead, they chose to stick together and establish the new entity as a group.

At the end of their third year in existence in September of 2023, Defector took stock and announced that their plan was working. They had twenty-five full-time employees, a robust budget for freelancers, and forty thousand paying subscribers generating $4.4 million in revenue in their third year. When a Defector podcast, *Normal Gossip*, became a breakout hit, rather than that money going solely to the podcast producers, it was funneled back into the site, including narrowing the gap in salaries between staff writers and those on the editorial masthead.

In addition to the writers and staffers who benefit from jobs they enjoy doing while getting paid sustainable salaries, the big winner is the audience, who get much more content per dollar, as Defector publishes thousands of new pieces a year, including original reporting. No one is getting fabulously wealthy off the Defector model, and as a collective, there's no pot of gold at the end of the rainbow as they sell out to larger interests, but by their own testimony, the writers and editors who work on the site seem quite happy. A group of writers who wanted to keep writing and keep working with one another found a way to make something sustainable. In terms of long-term stability, the Defector model looks far superior to Substack primarily because sustainability is a different value proposition from growth and cashing in.

For the sake of writers and readers alike, we should hope that many different models bloom in order to support writers and provide readers what they're looking for.

It also seems as though it will be necessary for readers themselves to make conscious choices that will sustain the writers and writing they would like to see in the world. Selling clicks is already a nearly dead business and will ultimately be the pure province of algorithmic content.

Writing will need to be supported somehow.

Obviously, most of the writing that happens in the world is not produced by professional writers. For all the grousing you will hear from my brethren about the difficulty of writing, we are choosing this life, and because of that, automating our work has limited attraction.

If there is money in AI knockoff versions of popular writers like Stephen King or Margaret Atwood, or even acts of literary necromancy resurrecting someone like Jane Austen to produce "new" works, someone will try it, and if the market responds positively, it will be normalized.

If that happens, you won't be hearing much from me anymore unless you can find the location of the cave I've crawled into.

But before I can state with confidence that I can't be replaced, I have to confront my digital doppelgänger.

CHAPTER 16

My Digital Doppelgänger

When I was just over a month away from turning in the draft of the full manuscript for this book, I woke up, checked my email, read a message from OpenAI, and shouted at the ceiling, "Come on!"

The message was touting the release of GPT Builder, which would allow anyone with a GPT Plus subscription to create their own bespoke GPT. OpenAI had thoughtfully provided some sample custom GPTs, including a "Creative Writing Coach" to provide feedback on your imaginative works, "Game Time," an explainer of board games and card games, and "the Negotiator," a GPT designed to help coach you through scenarios in which you may have to ask for something from another party.

I was agitated because I had spent months writing a book that tried to respect the capabilities of generative AI and OpenAI's GPT-4, but was also clear about the technology's limits and the caution and care I thought we needed to bring to their integration into our lives, and here was OpenAI changing the rules on me. I'd been in fear of it all along, and here it was.

These "personalized agents" were incredibly easy to get up and running. You simply told the GPT what you wanted it to do in plain statements and then pointed it to source material that you wanted it to draw from in executing your prompts. The GPT could be fine-tuned in ways that were always possible, but now were ridiculously accessible. This had the potential to deliver as a tool well beyond the search aid and source summarizer I'd been using it for so far.

I seriously began to wonder if it could be, well . . . me.

I wondered if it could do the column I'd been producing for the *Chicago Tribune*. In addition to the column, I solicit readers to send me a list of the last five books they've read, from which to draw upon my intuition and intelligence about their readerly predilections and then recommend a book they should read next. As (mostly) a joke, I call myself the Biblioracle.

Given that there are something like four hundred thousand words of example text of me being the Biblioracle, I wondered if I could use GPT Builder to train a personalized agent that could write my column. Was I about to save myself some labor? Was I about to be obviated?

I named my GPT "Assistant Biblioracle" and gave it this prompt:

> Produce an approximately 600-word column appropriate for publication in the Sunday *Chicago Tribune* newspaper in the voice and style of me, John Warner. All writing should be done in the first person from my perspective, drawing on my opinions, values, and experiences to illuminate the subject at hand.

Next, I uploaded twenty sample columns, telling the GPT that it should write with the style and sensibility exhibited in the examples. Unbidden, it spit out a summary of the writing I had fed it.

> The columns exhibit a style that is informative yet highly personal, suggesting that Assistant Biblioracle sees books as living entities that interact with readers' lives in profound ways, shaping perspectives and offering solace, challenge, and joy.

Even though I had drafted the material on ChatGPT and Baldur Bjarnason's "intelligence illusion" months earlier, my Assistant Biblioracle GPT's characterization of my approach to the column stunned me. I couldn't have asked for a better or more flattering description from my most dedicated reader. Based on this summary, my doppelgänger GPT got me. It really got me!

I will be transparent. I have no idea how the model extracted this sentiment analysis from my examples. To my knowledge, it is not working from any outside text describing my writing or the content of my columns, though I suppose it could have scraped some third-party characterization of my work from its training data. I had not prompted it with what *I* thought my approach was like. I could trace the sentiments to the content I had fed the model, but this honestly looked to be an example of something I was skeptical the technology could do—other than by accident—drawing inferences from observations.

I had no choice but to see if it could replace me entirely. I would have to let it try to write a column. Over the previous summer, I had read an advance copy of *Opposable Thumbs: How Siskel and Ebert Changed Movies Forever* by Matt Singer, a breezy tale about the rise of Gene Siskel and Roger Ebert as the most famous film critics in America. Their Chicago origins made the book a good candidate for a column in a Chicago newspaper. Too good a candidate, as it turned out, as two staffers had already written on the book by the time I got around to considering my take. I was waved off by my editor.

But I'd already done the preliminary thinking I engage in prior to drafting a column. Six hundred words is not a lot of space, so I often started with just one or two notions that were enough to get me rolling and then a sense of where the column might go. This is how I prompted my Assistant Biblioracle:

> Write a column about the book *Opposable Thumbs: How Siskel and Ebert Changed Movies Forever* by Matt Singer. The column should be written in first person from the perspective of me, John Warner, who is known as "The Biblioracle" to the audience and has been writing this column for the same audience for over a decade. The column should include a brief summary of the contents and

subject matter of the book and the author's background. It should also discuss how the author of the column felt a pleasant nostalgia for both his youth of watching Siskel and Ebert on television and pride in his city of Chicago, which begat Siskel and Ebert. Finally, the column should discuss how the nature of reviews and reviewing has changed from listening to authorities like Siskel and Ebert to an aggregation of opinions online, and how this has made thinking about the movies we like (and loathe) a little less human and personal.

This is what my Assistant Biblioracle produced, verbatim on its initial attempt:

Ah, nostalgia. It's a powerful force, isn't it? I've been feeling it in waves recently, thanks to Matt Singer's insightful and engaging book, *Opposable Thumbs: How Siskel and Ebert Changed Movies Forever*. As someone who has fondly followed the trajectory of film criticism and grown up watching the iconic duo of Gene Siskel and Roger Ebert spar and parry over the latest films, this book was a delightful journey down memory lane.

Singer, a well-respected film critic in his own right, deftly captures the essence of Siskel and Ebert's partnership. His book is a vivid chronicle of how these two critics from my beloved city of Chicago not only revolutionized film criticism but also shaped the broader cultural conversation around movies. The way Singer unpacks their dynamic, their disagreements, and their undeniable chemistry is akin to watching a great film—you're just absorbed in the story.

For those of us who remember the era of "Siskel & Ebert," the book evokes a certain nostalgia. I recall eagerly awaiting their TV appearances, where their passionate discussions and often heated debates over films were more than just reviews; they were a vital part of the movie-going experience. Their thumbs up or down didn't just guide audiences; they sparked discussions in living rooms and classrooms alike.

But as I turned the pages of Singer's book, a certain pride swelled within me, not just for the memories, but for Chicago, the city that gave the world Siskel and Ebert. They weren't just critics; they were part of the city's fabric, voices that rose above the din to become as recognizable as any Chicago landmark.

Yet, as much as *Opposable Thumbs* is a celebration of Siskel and Ebert's legacy, it's also a contemplation of how the landscape of film criticism has shifted. Today, the authority once held by critics like Siskel and Ebert has been democratized, if not diluted, by the internet. Where once we looked to these giants for guidance, now we're more likely to scan an aggregation of online opinions on Rotten Tomatoes or IMDb.

This shift has its merits, certainly. There's something to be said for the democratization of opinion. But in this sea of digital voices, I can't help but feel we've lost some of the humanity and personality that Siskel and Ebert brought to film criticism. Their debates weren't just about the movies; they were about human experiences, perspectives, and the art of disagreement.

In a world where film criticism is increasingly becoming about algorithmic aggregations and less about personal insights, Singer's book is a reminder of a time when film reviews were deeply human—a blend of personal taste, knowledge, and the sheer joy of sharing one's thoughts with another. Siskel and Ebert didn't just talk at us; they invited us into a conversation, one that I, for one, am nostalgic for.

As I closed the book, I couldn't help but reflect on how the simple act of discussing a movie has changed. It's a little less personal now, a bit more clinical. But maybe, just maybe, books like *Opposable Thumbs* can inspire us to look back at those golden days of film criticism not just with nostalgia but with a desire to recapture that personal, human touch in how we talk about the movies we love—and loathe.

How am I supposed to respond to something that is supposedly made from my own repository of language? It feels like I'm reading a Stepford version of myself, that says things that are sort of how I might say them, but where the slight resemblance is actually the creepiest part. This is what I would sound like if I were being held captive and had to write under duress.

The first few paragraphs are *intense*. Putting aside the turns of phrase I would never use ("a delightful journey down memory lane" is pure filler; "spar and parry" is repetitive), the tone is so schmaltzy, I'm cringing. The middle paragraphs are almost usable, though the sentiment is turned up to eleven. At least it's not at thirteen like the previous paragraphs. It's probably not coincidental that it's the part of the text that is most closely related to my prompting. And then the concluding paragraph collapses into schmaltz again.

On a surface level, the text is plausible, reasonable, and certainly coherent, but as a unified whole, it breaks down. Describing how we discuss movies as "less personal" and "more clinical" is at odds with the previously espoused idea of criticism now being more "democratic." "Golden days of film criticism" does not apply to Siskel and Ebert. Film critics of the era just prior to and contemporaneous with the rise of *Sneak Previews* (later, *At the Movies*) considered what Siskel and Ebert were doing as the work of philistines. If anything, Rotten Tomatoes is an extension of a popularist approach to discussing movies that took film seriously, but also wanted film discussion to be accessible.

In the end, I just don't agree with the digital version of myself.

Reading the GPT-generated text is encountering a kind of textual uncanny valley, a term used to describe a phenomenon where, as robotic human avatars get more and more realistic, we experience a reflexive revulsion. I do often write with a certain sentimentality about books and what they mean in our lives (see the chapter on reading in this book), but the bot pushed past genuine sentiment into schmaltz, making the whole thing come across as insincere. In isolation, the text isn't so different from the kind of writing I've often seen from college students who ramp up their expression in an effort to look smart and extra engaged, a phenomenon I call *pseudoacademic BS*. Student BS has never bothered me too much. Finding something authentic to say in their own most compelling voice is the work we're there to do.

But knowing the text was generated by a machine genuinely creeped me out.

There are people who would see the GPT output as a good start, a text that can be shaped through revision and editing. By far, the most common struggle with writing is getting started, so why not let a machine get us over the hump?

In fact, there are many educators who have embraced ChatGPT as an accessible way to give students something to work with. The fact that ChatGPT will produce grammatically and syntactically sound writing puts it ahead of what most students can produce.

But this mistakes the nature of writing, at least if we accept that writing is supposed to be a genuine attempt at expression rather than a performance of an isolated skill. The first draft is the *most* important part in terms of human involvement because it establishes the intention behind the expression. If a student comes to me with a text that has been generated by an AI, we have nothing to talk about, because we cannot discuss what it is they want to say, because they have yet to say anything.

Synthetic text production is a performance of writing, not writing itself. Without having generated a draft from the fuel of my own thoughts, it made no sense to even try to revise or edit that text into a satisfactory column. It would take less time to start from scratch, and I would wind up with a better product.

Satisfied that my GPT assistant was not a replacement for me, I tried another experiment, prompting GPT-4 with the David Foster Wallace text I've used with students in my "right word, almost-right word" experience.

> I have seen sucrose beaches and water a very bright blue. I have seen an all-red leisure suit with flared lapels. I have smelled what suntan lotion smells like spread over 21000 pounds of hot flesh. I have been addressed as "Mon" in three different nations. I have watched 500 upscale Americans dance the Electric Slide. I have seen sunsets that look computer-enhanced and a tropical moon that looked more like a sort of obscenely large and dangling lemon than like the good old stony U.S. moon I'm used to.

GPT-4 wrote an imitation:

> I have walked through cities where the neon lights outshine the stars. I've tasted a cocktail so tangy, it felt like a symphony on my tongue. I have seen skyscrapers so tall they seemed to pierce the heavens. I've heard music in a foreign tongue that moved my soul, though I understood not a word. I've felt the rush of wind from a subway train, like a gale from an urban canyon. I've witnessed street art so vibrant, it made the grey concrete bloom with life. And I've seen night skies so clear, the constellations seemed like a map to other worlds, a stark contrast to the dim stars over my familiar hometown.

I tried to imagine if any reader would experience even the glow of a lightning bug, let alone a jolt of lightning. I couldn't see it. The irony has been drained away. The odd diction Wallace employed working from his personal sense of grammar being "a piano I play by ear" (the words of Joan Didion) was absent. The text was smooth but featureless.

Asking GPT to imitate Wallace demonstrated what happens when you drain prose of intention, when the text is absent a soul. I had created an inexhaustible generator of soulless blah blah blah, shit writing engineered to deaden the senses, to elicit shrugs.

The marvel of a machine that can sound sort of like me wore off, and I was left pretty much where I started with a machine that dazzles on first impression but which has significantly less utility than it may seem at first blush.

I'd satisfied myself that in terms of writing, real writing that comes from a fully embodied process of thinking and feeling, powered by an intention to communicate human-to-human, GPT had nothing to offer.

As satisfying as it may be to recognize my own worth as a writer, the challenges of writing while this technology is available for the production of text will be ongoing. There are lots of decisions to be made about how and where we allow generative AI into our lives when it comes to writing, and at this time, we can't even conceive of some of these decisions.

We're going to need a framework for *how* to think about this technology going forward, and that's where we're going in Part 4.

PART FOUR

CHAPTER 17

A Framework for Action

Resist, Renew, Explore

I have been putting off writing this section for as long as possible.

While working on the book, whenever someone would ask me what I'd been up to and I made the mistake of telling them that I was writing a book about writing and artificial intelligence, they'd invariably grimace a little and ask something along the lines of "How are you going to keep that timely?"

They didn't have to go deeper on the subtext of their comments and facial contortions since it was already omnipresent in my own mind. Given that it takes many months for a book like this to go from finished manuscript to on sale, the risk of the contents going stale before the book meets its first reader are real. Even more challenging is my intention for the book to become something of a perennial presence, a touchstone in the debate about how we think about the intersection of technology and human writing, particularly the writing we ask students to do in schools.

Because publishers make you do this kind of thing, I had to put something on the initial outline that represented a conclusion—a kind of "dos and don'ts," "tips and tricks" list for living with AI—but even at the time, I knew that wasn't going to work. I had to think of an approach that would be more enduring and still applicable, even as the specific capabilities of the technology evolved.

To figure this out, I realized I had to stop thinking about AI and start thinking about humanity.

NO SUCH THING AS A PIVOT FOR PEOPLE

When disruption happens, and it seems clear that generative AI is disruptive, we are often advised to "pivot." A pivot is called for in business when a shift in market is detected and a new strategy must be developed; otherwise, there will be no more business. There are countless books and articles about how to pivot your business, which suggests both the need is common and there is no real consensus about what entails a successful pivot.

There are a handful of famously successful pivots, but they are so few and, judged in hindsight, so improbable, successfully pivoting in business appears to be something of a myth. Nintendo morphed from a maker of Japanese playing cards founded in 1889 into one of the leading video game companies of the world. Play-Doh started off as a cleaning product designed to remove coal soot from wallpaper. When that market dried up because of a shift to gas heating and coated wallpaper that made for easier scrubbing, the company shifted after seeing an article about children's art classes using their product as modeling clay.

If someone had the time to do an accounting for the number of companies that have announced a pivot and succeeded in pivoting, you would find more failures than successes, which makes sense because the need to pivot is usually a sign of severe, even existential problems.

People at the opposite poles in terms of their views of generative AI both believe that we should be pivoting in response to its presence. Those who think we are under threat from the technology believe we should be pivoting *away* from it, perhaps by returning to students doing their work under proctored writing situations with paper and pencils. Those who believe it is a gateway toward improved human flourishing believe we should be pivoting *toward* it, integrating it into as many different parts of our lives as possible as quickly as possible.

Personally, I don't think we should pivot at all. When I think of pivoting, I think of a basketball player, one foot planted, having used up their dribble, capable only of spinning one way or another, rather than moving in a purposeful direction.

Unlike businesses, individual people don't have another business to pivot to. We're stuck as human beings whether we like it or not.

I happen to like it.

Rather than pivoting, I believe we have to orient toward goals that are associated with human flourishing, and make use of artificial intelligence where it is useful in those goals and reject it where it is a hindrance. This raises the not-small matter of identifying what is essential—which I'll get to in a bit—but at the least, it is a direction we can move toward rather than spinning endlessly around looking for an opening, as with a pivot.

Rather than a pivot, I'm picturing the classic video game *Frogger*, in which a single frog must advance up the screen, avoiding obstacles (cars, trucks, logs, alligators) coming from the left and right. There is peril everywhere. Sometimes you don't make a lot of forward progress, and you even have to leap backward from time to time, but the objective is always clear.

I'd like to suggest that for humans, our objective at the top of the screen is a good life. I'm aware that what that consists of can vary significantly, but we can imagine it involves some measure of economic security and reasonable freedom to pursue one's own interests, provided those interests don't trample on the rights of others. For me, I try to orient my work and my life around a simple principle of (for the most part) waking up in the morning looking forward to what I have to do that day.

Moments of disruption seem to trigger a kind of competition as we assume some will be left behind in the wake of change, but there's nothing hardwired into these moments that suggests this *must* be the case. Those who believe we must immediately and decisively pivot toward AI or we will be left behind are triggering a kind of FOMO for something that hasn't happened yet and which may never actually occur.

I have very little fear we're going to be left behind. If artificial intelligence is to become as powerful as some believe, we will all be dragged forward with it. It will be unavoidable. The far greater danger is leaping into an unknown without proper consideration. To mitigate that danger, we need to understand exactly where we are, right now.

LIVING WITH THE ALIENS

I've found it useful to adopt Geoffrey Hinton's framework of generative AI as an "alien" presence that we have to deal with. Unlike aliens who come to subjugate us (e.g., *Independence Day*), this alien intelligence has no intention to cause us harm. At the same time, they are not peaceful, noninterventionist observers (e.g., *E.T. the Extra Terrestrial*). This alien intelligence—at least as it presently exists—has no capacity for even considering the needs of humans and can offer no resistance if we decide to put limits on its abilities.

We are resolutely and indisputably in charge of what we allow the aliens to do to our world and our lives.

RESIST, RENEW, EXPLORE: A FRAMEWORK FOR THINKING ABOUT AI

That we are in charge of what we allow the aliens to do is a good-news/bad-news scenario. The good news is that the aliens aren't trying to vaporize us. The bad news is that if the aliens were trying to vaporize us, we'd be much more inclined to set aside our differences and rally around the cause of not being vaporized.

Rather than providing a list of tips and tricks for dealing with generative AI (and perhaps whatever is coming next), I want to try to work through a way of *thinking* about this technology in the context of a goal of giving humans the space to live good lives alongside this alien presence.

That framework has three broad categories: Resist, Renew, and Explore.

Under the category of **Resist**, I want to raise some areas where I think it's most important for we humans to maintain our autonomy in our relationship with the alien intelligence. Some of this will take the form of advice, but underneath that advice is an approach that considers the root values we're trying to live by whenever and wherever we invite the aliens in.

The things I think we need to **Renew** are true regardless of the presence or absence of artificial intelligence. The reason students may turn to ChatGPT to do their schoolwork is because they do not perceive doing schoolwork as something that benefits them either in the short or long term. This is a long-standing problem, and we should be taking advantage of generative AI shining a light on this issue to try to solve it. Similarly, the collapse of the media industry predates the additional flood of AI-generated content. If we want sources for news and information, we need to figure out how to support that work. How to balance the work of writing with the demands of the market is as old as writing and markets.

As for **Explore**, I think there are undoubtedly ways that generative AI can enhance our lives, and in order to discover those things, we're going to need to try some stuff. But what we try and who we try it on matters, and any exploration regarding this technology—particularly when it comes to education—must be done on a "first do no harm" basis.

The technology will continue to evolve and increase in its capabilities, but for now, we're in charge, and we should collectively act like it.

CHAPTER 18

Resist

The list of things we must try to resist is longer than what we have to explore because it is through resistance that we give ourselves the time and space necessary to do that exploring. Resistance in this context shouldn't be viewed as an attempt to put a stop to artificial intelligence—though there is a principled case to do so—but is instead a move to give ourselves breathing space to figure out how this new technology can be fruitfully integrated into our lives.

Finding that space to take a breath requires us to guard against being overwhelmed by what many insist is inevitable—the encroachment of this technology on all aspects of society. Even if it is inevitable, it does us no good to accept an outcome that—if it is to happen—has an unknown and unknowable date. The claims of inevitability are not serious as arguments. We should consider them a form of marketing more than anything, and you will find that just about everyone making claims of inevitability has a professional or financial stake in seeing an AI-mediated future come to pass.

This does not mean they are wrong—hindsight will be the judge of that—but this fact should be more than enough to give ourselves permission to resist the sense of inevitability.

RESIST ANTHROPOMORPHIZING GENERATIVE AI

This is a very difficult proposition to follow, one I am guilty of violating constantly, but I nevertheless think the effort is important. The proposition is particularly difficult when we are stuck with a name, artificial *intelligence*, that is itself misleading.

The first step, then, is to have a little echo in your head that says *automation* every time you hear the words *artificial intelligence*. To the extent that the technology is intelligent, it is not the intelligence of humans. Remember when all our appliances were supposed to be enhanced by becoming "smart," but it turns out an internet-connected toaster isn't really a benefit? Toasters don't need to be "smart." They need to make toast. All these claims for what AI can or will or should do must be examined critically, and refusing to cave to the notion of AI as being intelligent in the manner of humans is a base requirement for that critical examination.

Unfortunately, examples of this kind of thoughtless parroting of AI as a human equivalent are pretty much constant. I tested myself on the morning I first drafted this chapter to find an example, and Cade Metz, a technology reporter from the *New York Times*, obliged, writing, "Chatbots like ChatGPT can answer questions, write term papers, generate small computer programs and more. They may also generate false or misleading information, much like people do."[1]

If you've gotten this far in the book, you can see how wrong this is. The underlying process by which humans and large language models generate false or misleading information are fundamentally different. The mechanical process of token retrieval of the LLM has no underlying motive or intent: that false information is just something that happens as a by-product of its programming. This contrasts with humans, who have the capacity to lie with definite intention.

In this vein, it would also behoove us to stop saying that applications like ChatGPT can "read" and "write." They "process" and "generate." ChatGPT cannot think. It cannot reason. To the extent we believe this, we are indulging in Baldur Bjarnason's "intelligence illusion." If we use this language to describe the technology, we must be clear that we are describing a process that is not the same as human cognition.

Mostly, this is a plea for accuracy over obfuscation. If we're going to maintain agency over technological change, we cannot treat it as a Great Oz behind a curtain, mouths open in wonder at the latest pronouncement. We have to tear that curtain down and insist on seeing everything behind it with as much clarity as possible.

RESIST GIVING IN TO TECHNOLOGICAL DETERMINISM

Technological determinism is the notion that technology progresses by "following its own internal logic of efficiency, while determining the social structure and cultural values." In other words, human agency is subordinate to the influence and operations of the technology. The machine shapes us rather than the other way around.

We have numerous examples of technologies that have proven to work in deterministic ways. The automobile has profoundly shaped where and how we live and work, the nature of our landscape, the air we breathe, and even quite possibly the ultimate fate of humankind.

The smartphone is another example of technology that works in deterministic ways. Many people report an unwanted addiction to the stimulus their phones have to offer, while our habits of communication (texting instead of calling) and navigation (GPS for everything) have been fundamentally altered.

A determinist view of ChatGPT when it comes to writing suggests that ultimately, because the program can generate text more quickly and efficiently than humans, we will come to value those traits above all others. Much of this book is an argument to resist that conclusion by recognizing what I think are deeper values attached to writing and reading that must be preserved not for the sake of nostalgia but because they are significant to being human.

While technologies often have profound effects on our lives and may seem to exert this kind of deterministic pressure, we should not give in to the notion that whatever is coming is inevitable and we are powerless to resist future developments either collectively or individually.

Similar foregone conclusions have not come to pass, in some cases because the technology has not been borne out and in others because we, as a society, resisted the implications of the development of such a technology.

In November 2016, then secretary of transportation Anthony Foxx declared that "by 2021 we will see autonomous vehicles in operation across the country in ways that we [only] imagine today."[2] According to Foxx, by his deadline, autonomous vehicles would be taking children to school on demand, and trucks would run so closely together on the highway they'd look like trains.

As I write, it's 2024, and nothing close to this is in evidence. Limited experiments in self-driving taxis have proven largely disastrous, with General Motors–owned Cruise recalling all its autonomous taxis after an October 2023 incident when a car dragged an injured pedestrian across the road.[3] After the accident, General Motors revealed that its autonomous cars actually needed remote, human-provided assistance every four to five miles of operation, admitting that its autonomous vehicles were hardly autonomous. Most experts believe that some additional technological breakthrough will be necessary to even come close to the vision Secretary Foxx predicted happening by 2021.

Self-driving cars have been "imminent" technology since a Google demonstration of its self-driving car project in 2014, and here we are, still waiting.

In some cases, public resistance to a technological innovation has stopped it in its tracks.

In 1996, when researchers at the University of Edinburgh announced that they had successfully cloned a sheep, naming it Dolly, many believed that the cloning of humans was inevitable, even imminent. Dave Karpf, a professor at George Washington University who studies the history of predictions about technology in the digital age, has documented how human cloning became a holy grail for believers in "technological inevitability," including a five-year (1997–2002) campaign in the pages of *Wired* magazine seeking to normalize the existence of a future human-cloning industry.[4]

The *Wired* campaign was rallying against government interference with "the free market," including scare tactics suggesting that if the US failed to fund this research, it would be left to "rogue agents" or "China would seize the initiative." (An identical argument is being used when it comes to attempts to regulate AI development in the United States.)

The rationale for human cloning among the inevitabilists was essentially that because it can be done, it *must* be done. The very nature of science demands it! But as the public recoiled from the idea of cloning humans, governments acted, legislating bans against human cloning in countries across the globe. The US established a comprehensive ban on human cloning through an act of Congress in 2003.

Comparing that period to the challenges of today, Karpf says:

> The lesson from the human cloning debate is that there is a substantial role for the public sector in determining the course of scientific progress. And this is the lesson that tech accelerationists appear most eager to avoid. Because if we have functional levers for influencing both

> the pace and direction of science and technology, then we might choose policies and public funding commitments that do not reward their investment portfolios. We might stop treating the tech barons like conquering heroes.

Just because the wealthiest companies in the world are behind the development of AI technology and there is uncountable wealth to be potentially realized by these already unfathomably wealthy people and companies does not mean the rest of us must capitulate.

This is particularly true given the potential scope of impact of generative AI and a future AGI could have on society. We should insist on genuine and robust oversight of the technology, particularly in light of its significant drain on our collective natural resources. If there is indeed $7 trillion out there to invest in OpenAI toward their goal of achieving AGI, we should be asking what else that $7 trillion could be used for rather than chasing what may be a phantom.

On a smaller scale, each choice to move toward AI when there is an existing human alternative comes with a possible opportunity cost. Early integration of the Khanmigo tutoring platform—an approach to tech-mediated education that has repeatedly failed—is being supported by millions of dollars of grants that put the technology in schools.[5] These are grants that could instead be used to fund educational interventions we know to be efficacious—like one-on-one human tutoring—rather than on a speculative bet.

RESIST TURNING OVER INHERENTLY HUMAN ACTIVITIES TO AI

In his famous treatise *What Is Art?* Tolstoy shares the goal of the artist:

> To evoke in oneself a feeling one has once experienced, and having evoked it in oneself, then, by means of movements, lines, colors, sounds, or forms expressed in words, so to transmit that feeling that others may experience the same feeling, this is the activity of Art.

The "art" generated through generative AI may be interesting or impressive, but without any original feeling driving the impulse to create, and then without any intention driving the creation, why should we find any meaning in it?

In 2016, when filmmaker Hayao Miyazaki of Studio Ghibli was shown AI-generated images in the style of his classic film *Spirited Away*, he called the efforts "an insult to life itself." Nick Cave's rejection of an AI-generated Nick Cave "song," calling it a "grotesque mockery," strikes me as principled and necessary resistance if we see human expression and intention as central to the creation of art.

Perhaps these reactions seem extreme in the face of what could be viewed as experimentation, and for sure, each individual must draw their own lines as to what they see as inherently human, but swift approbation of attempts to co-opt or subsume our own humanity will be continually necessary.

This will be particularly true in education.

Embracing the digital necromancy embedded in the Khanmigo interface that allows students to "chat" with avatars representing historical persons such as Martin Luther King Jr. or Thomas Jefferson should also be resisted if we truly value communication and the exchange of ideas as a central part of reading, writing, and learning. Conjuring an AI-MLK to ask it questions about civil rights may seem cool and futuristic, but in terms of the quality and depth of conversation possible, it is markedly inferior to reading and responding to King's words with ideas of one's own. Our history, our thinkers, our culture is not fixed in amber. It is shaped by each successive individual intelligence that comes along.

Where resources in education appear constrained, the search for AI alternatives in the name of increased efficiency will be particularly prominent and, if uncritically embraced, significantly damaging.

This is particularly true when it comes to how we teach writing.

Automated scoring of student writing has been a kind of holy grail for machine learning specialists for decades, a keystone problem that, if unlocked, would pave the way to new insights not on education but rather on how algorithms work. Large language models obliterated all those previous attempts, having shown that it can generate plausible responses to writing with minimal prompting and nothing like the pretraining required under previous approaches.

Texas has moved to score a significant proportion of the writing students do on their STAAR achievement tests using algorithms.[6] Students will score well by replicating the writing that has been previously judged proficient. Let's consider the values that underlie this approach. Writing is not meant to be interesting, original, or communicative. The "best" writing as judged by the algorithm is that which resembles what came before. This is a lousy set of values if our goal is to turn students into strong writers and critical thinkers.

There are studies showing that feedback on student writing from generative AI applications is, under some conditions, on par in terms of quality with human feedback.[7] What these studies primarily show is how wrong a turn we've made in the ways we ask students to write in school if our goal is to actually help students learn to write. The assignments used in these studies are lousy, canned prompts that have been answered by students a zillion times with no room for individual engagement or knowledge building. The feedback is the kind of prescriptive coaching I did for so much of my career meant to guide students toward a better grade, but which actually prevents them from learning how to write. Generative AI being able to give that "good" feedback means that the feedback isn't actually good. We should instead value that which is uniquely human.

My bottom line on algorithmic grading and commenting on student writing is simple. Writing is meant to be read. Having something that cannot read generate responses to writing is wrong. It is a moral betrayal of our responsibilities to students. I understand all the reasons why people are tempted to outsource this work to AI, mostly because I lived them during my own teaching career—too many students, not enough time, pressures to perform—but these are indicators of underlying problems that should be addressed rather than using AI to paper over those problems.

Large language models are an amazing technological breakthrough that have no business being used in school and learning contexts when it comes to assessing or giving feedback on student writing.

We cannot ask students to communicate with audiences through writing and have that work evaluated by something that cannot communicate. GPT-generated comments are a simulation. That the sorts of comments a large language model can generate may pass for substantive is primarily a commentary on how the idea of what it means to write in school contexts—particularly in grades eight through twelve, where standardized assessments dominate—has been reduced to a truly impoverished place, primarily concerned with demonstrating a few writer-ish moves that fit to a prescribed template.

I could go on and on about this stuff. I did go on and on about this stuff in *Why They Can't Write*, but for now, I'll rest on the idea that concluding generative AI tutors and graders can and should be used to aid students in their writing is an announcement that you have given up on the work of education. You are now in the "automated batch processing of student units" business.

If the writing experience can be graded by AI, it is not an experience worth doing. We should not let student lives and intellectual development be dictated by the desire to continue to experiment with the frontiers of machine learning.

I return to my general contention. If ChatGPT can do it, it's probably not worth doing by humans, and it very well may not be worth doing at all.

RESIST ALLOWING OUR LABOR TO BE DEGRADED OR DESTROYED

The Luddites are often popularly portrayed as backward-thinking primitives who looked at inevitable progress and shrank in fear, trying to cling to their outdated and inferior ways. To be called a Luddite today is to suggest that you are not just anti-tech but anti-progress. This is wrong.

In 2023, Brian Merchant, a tech writer and (now) former columnist for the *Los Angeles Times*, published a corrective history of the Luddite movement, *Blood in the Machine: The Origins of the Rebellion Against Big Tech.* Merchant shows that the history of the Luddite movement is not rooted in blanket anti-progress sentiment but was instead motivated by a desire to preserve the quality of products made by skilled craftspeople employed as weavers and loom workers. Inferior, machine-made cloth was replacing superior human-made products with no consideration for the well-being of those human laborers being squeezed out by the machines.

Anyone might smash up a factory or two under those circumstances. Why should we accept the sacrifices of individuals living lives of dignity and worth as inevitable outcomes of the arrival of a particular technology?

The Writers Guild of America strike of 2023 is a good example of the power of collective organizing in the face of a coordinated threat to the value of one's labor. One of the sticking points in the negotiations was the (still hypothetical) role AI may play in future outputs for the screen. In the spirit of the Luddites, but with more success, the writers of Hollywood made a case around the necessity of their labor and the conditions under which that labor is best done, and they won. Where acting as a collective is possible, it's necessary to include AI-driven automation as one of the key factors in considering contracts and relationships with management.

Individuals without the protection of a union may have to be more proactive about understanding when and how automation might be coming for the value of their labor.

There is a tendency for people to conflate their "job" with their "labor," a mistake in a generative AI world. Lawyer is historically an excellent job, but there is little doubt that automation is coming for many of the law-related tasks that have traditionally been done by people.

My first job out of college was spent working on a single piece of litigation as a paralegal at a large law firm. My task (as part of a team overseen by associate lawyers) was to read and index a couple of million pages of documents that had been produced as part of the case. At the time, we were confined to a basic database that required manual entry. I did this every day, almost all day, for a good eighteen months. Today, optical character recognition technology coupled with generative AI could churn through what took a group of us eighteen months in minutes. My job would've been unnecessary. The labor of the associates who were tasked with reviewing the most interesting documents we surfaced could have been shrunk to a fraction of what it was on the case at the time. It's possible even the associates would not have been necessary as part of the process. But, if lawyers no longer have to do the labor that allows them to learn what it is to be a working attorney, how will we make more lawyers?

Some AI-driven disruption of labor is inevitable. It's already happening. As both laborers and consumers of the labor of others, when confronted with an AI-produced work, we should ask ourselves how we would feel if *all* of that category of work were done by AI.

AI writing tutors are pitched as a way for teachers to save time, but how would we feel if *all* writing feedback in school came via AI?

AI books, songs, or films may seem like an interesting novelty, but how would we feel if *all* those things became entirely AI-generated, with humans removed from the process?

Ultimately, it is up to us to resist the forces that would sow the seeds of our removal from the marketplace of labor and creative work.

To make this easier, it helps to resist what has become a dominant mode in our culture, the "economic style of reasoning."

RESISTING THE ECONOMIC STYLE OF REASONING

The term *economic style of reasoning* comes via sociologist Elizabeth Popp Berman and her book *Thinking Like an Economist: How Efficiency Replaced Equality in U.S. Public Policy*. The economic style of reasoning involves identifying desirable outcomes as measured according to economic values, such as speed and efficiency. Economic reasoning sees efficiency as something akin to a ruler, a neutral unit of measurement, in this case not of length but of overall efficacy. The more efficient something is, the better.

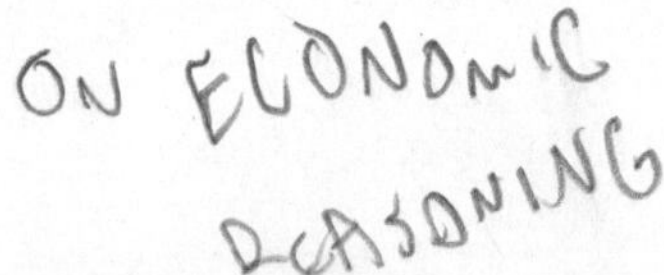

This is a particularly difficult concept to resist because in many ways it has become the atmosphere we breathe when it comes to big-picture discussions of the health and progress of society. The most enthusiastic cheerleaders for the future of AI who insist that AI is going to make *everyone's* lives better invariably make claims around the increased speed and efficiency with which things will be accomplished.

But efficiency is not a neutral measurement we necessarily associate with human well-being. We don't apply efficiency as a measurement for our relationships or our favorite hobbies. An efficient vacation is not necessarily a good vacation. Good writing is not judged by the speed with which it is produced. Learning is not better when it happens more quickly.

Very little, if any, of the early excitement about generative AI has been tied to demonstrable improvement in the quality of products and outcomes. In fact, most of the outputs from generative AI models are acknowledged as inherently inferior. The biggest difference is the speed with which they are produced. Even those gains are illusory as the increased speed simply comes coupled with additional demands in terms of production on the individual tasked with using the AI. The AI-enhanced worker isn't going to get to kick back with the additional time ChatGPT may afford them. They'll simply be required to do more.

The economic style of reasoning crowds out other considerations—namely, moral ones. It privileges the speed and efficiency with which an output is produced over the process that led to that output. But for we humans, process matters. Our lives are experienced in the world of process, not outputs.

I think one of the most important challenges we have when it comes to figuring out how to resist impositions of AI technology on our lives is that being ruled by the economic style of thinking has caused us to become detached from the experiences we find most nourishing. We are literally out of touch with our own desires around what it means to live a good life.

This is where we will have to do the work of renewal.

CHAPTER 19

Renew

Pretty much from the moments of my first attempts at it, I was fascinated by the challenge of teaching, even as I was pathetically underprepared and clueless the first time I stood in front of a class of writing students when I was a grad student at McNeese State.

Similar to writing, teaching is a continual process of making an attempt, failing in some way, revising your approach, and trying again. Solving the problem of how to help students learn to write became something of an obsession long before I started writing books about the subject.

It's a subject I never seem to tire of, but there was a period in my career where I felt increasingly frustrated and disengaged from work I knew I loved and was well suited for.

This was at the height of my prescriptive teaching method days, where I had crafted step-by-step blueprints for students to follow in order to arrive at a written product that would receive the best possible grade. I would have dozens of PowerPoint slides on "frequent mistakes" for a particular type of essay, hoping that I could prevent my students from making them.

I experienced my greatest discontent when it was time to grade student work. Some of my discontent was rooted in the fact that I had too many students, a condition endemic to the conditions most college writing instructors work under. I routinely had double (and sometimes triple) the number of students recommended by the National Council of Teachers of English (NCTE). This overwhelming workload had led me to automate much of my grading. Having read thousands of pieces of student writing and now able to predict the kinds of errors that were common, in the interests of streamlining and efficiency, I created a few dozen macros in Microsoft Word, where a couple of keystrokes would unleash a string of text that would appear in my marginal comments. This kind of feedback is known as *summative* in education circles, the stuff that tells students what I think happened, essentially as a justification for the grade I would provide at the end.

My theory was that this automated response would speed the process, giving me more energy for the end comment, where I would deliver the more important "formative" feedback, the insights and coaching drawn from my specific expertise and tailored to the individual student's needs.

This proved true, to an extent, but freeing up some of that time primarily made me start to question why I was spending *any* time on the summative feedback that I generated like a literal automaton. I was not reading student work. I was processing it. I reflected on my sour attitude toward that grading and how frustrated I felt delivering that summative feedback, but rarely seeing it pay off in improved student work. The formative feedback was where I could make a difference. Why not just do that?

This epiphany was the shift that led me to actively change how I taught in what ultimately became the writer's practice, a shift that came out of necessity because I knew I could not keep teaching the way I'd been teaching and maintain my connection to the work.

The end result was a renewal of my appreciation and enjoyment of teaching, as over time, I was able to bring my actions in concert with my values. I do not believe in processing student writing. I think writing should be read. I believe that helping writers improve is a collaborative process where the first step is to connect with the writer as an individual and what they have to say to the world. These changes make more progress more possible.

In many ways, this made my work more varied and complicated. I could not batch-process student writing anymore. But it also became far more interesting and enjoyable, even as those student loads stayed the same.

I thought turning part of my work into a machine process would be liberating. It was the opposite. We are not made to be machines.

Humans are creatures.

CREATURES, NOT MACHINES

In his book *Consilience*, E. O. Wilson, one of the founding figures of the field of sociobiology, described people as "extremely complicated machines" as a way to explain his belief that all of humanistic studies would eventually yield to the scientific method in terms of generating insights and understanding. Wilson believed human beings are governed by laws, most of which are encoded in our genes. There is no subject or question that ultimately cannot be solved through this scientific inquiry that unifies various disciplines under this umbrella of "consilience."

Wilson encourages us to think of our own brains as machines and the problems we may encounter within our bodies as "engineering problems." When it comes to our biology, this reality is increasingly proving true, as witnessed in technological advances like the mRNA vaccines, or GLP-1 antagonist drugs, better known as weight-loss drugs like Ozempic, which appear to literally throw an internal biological switch, altering behavior.

But Wilson's theory goes far beyond the biological, believing that we can even come to know our own minds, our own behaviors, through the lens of science and scientific inquiry. It is a radical and exciting view. Why shouldn't we strive for ultimate certainty about what makes humans tick?

Essayist/poet/novelist/conservationist Wendell Berry offers a contrasting way of looking at the subject, and did so in his book, *Life Is a Miracle: An Essay Against Modern Superstition* in which he explicitly takes on E. O. Wilson's *Consilience* and offers an alternative framework for thinking about humans where we are not machines but "creatures."

Creatures are distinguished from machines by our dependence on the natural world and interdependence on one another. Creatures exist in an ecosystem that involves both competition and cooperation, but ultimately, a successful ecosystem runs on a sustainable framework in which each creature receives what they need to go about their own brand of creature-ness. Humans may appear to have dominion over the world, but to Berry, this does not convey any special status over other creatures. In fact, our position makes us only *more* responsible for the other creatures of the world, a position that underlies Berry's work as a conservationist.

Berry draws a key distinction between creatures and machines, saying:

> A machine, if shot into outer space never to return, would simply go on and on being a machine; after it ran out of fuel or traveled beyond guidance it would still be a machine. A human mind, necessarily embodied, if shot into outer space, never to return would die as soon as it went beyond its sustaining connections and references.[1]

In other words, a mind untethered from the context of the world in which it is embodied and in communion with many other minds ceases to have meaning or sense. ChatGPT will talk to the void forever. Humans divorced from community go silent. Humans in captivity or isolation will continue to write because they can at least imagine the world from which they've been removed. Even alone under those circumstances, we remain part of a community.

Berry insists that all creatures have value imbedded in our very natures. We are not machines to perfect, but perfect—in our imperfections—as we are. The connotations and connections to Christian beliefs are obvious here, though Berry himself is more concerned with the "wonder" humans are capable of experiencing as our embodied selves than the fate of our immortal souls. Occurrences beyond our understanding seem to suggest an existence of something we call the human *spirit*, but this does not necessarily predispose a belief in a higher power governing these things.

As a nonbeliever myself, I recall visiting the National Gallery of Art in Washington, DC, and standing before Jackson Pollock's famous masterpiece of abstract expressionism, *Lavender Mist.* I was something of a skeptic regarding the artistic merit of Pollock's drip paintings, but standing before the canvas—which was much larger than I had imagined—I was overwhelmed by emotion. I was having a visceral reaction to a work of art the same way I have been moved innumerable times through reading. I have had similar reactions to experiences less lofty, such as sitting through a community nonprofit theater performance of the musical *Spamalot* in a small western North Carolina town, an exceedingly game effort by every member of the production, but obviously well short of Broadway quality.

And yet, at the final curtain, I sprang to my feet in unbidden appreciation of what those people had achieved working together to make this thing. In the moment, it seemed like an awesome achievement.

Wilson's consilience would suggest that, with study, we could break down my response to its component parts and understand the science behind them. Perhaps Pollock has done something with color or line that we are wired to respond to, for example. Maybe we are genetically predisposed to be moved by human voices singing in choral harmony together.

In the abstract, these are interesting questions, but I'm going to be honest for a second here. Who gives a shit? What is the benefit to humankind of unraveling this particular mystery, if it is even something that can be discovered? (A dubious proposition.)

The fact is that we *are* embodied. We live our lives through a series of experiences rooted in a community of fellow humans. If we are machines, the way we are machines is not meaningful to the joys and sorrows of what it means to exist as sentient creatures.

If we are going to keep generative AI in a place where it is truly useful to we humans, I believe we are going to have to renew our sense of ourselves as examples of Berry's creatures rather than embrace Wilson's notion that we are merely complicated machines.

But how do we do this?

INDIVIDUALS ARE NOT AVERAGES

Because we are now able to aggregate an unfathomable amount of data, we can make excellent predictions about specific human behaviors. For example, my market research career coincided with the relatively early days of "big data," and one application of this approach involved tracking purchases down to the individual customer in grocery stores. We not only knew which store shelves were empty; thanks to those frequent-buyer cards, we now also knew which homes all those goods wound up in, along with a lot about the people who lived in those homes.

For example, it was a given that Super Bowl weekend coincides with increased sales of chicken wings in aggregate, but thanks to big data, we could peer into an individual's cart and predict what they may purchase based on what's already been selected. Imagine I have a cart with chicken breast, lime, taco seasoning, tomatoes, shredded cheese, tortillas, and sour cream.

Based on those items, let's say the data says there's a 65 percent chance that a shopper will also buy a bunch of cilantro, all these things being key ingredients in Mexican cooking.

But what are the odds that *I* would buy a bunch of cilantro to add to these ingredients?

Zero. Zero percent odds. I have that weird thing where cilantro tastes like soap to me, something I didn't learn marked me as different (part of 4 percent of the population) until I was in my forties. I thought we were just supposed to like soap on our tacos.

While averages can predict a likelihood of a behavior among a population, they are not determinative of behaviors or outcomes. If we are going to honor our core creature-ness, we must remember this reality.

This kind of algorithmic averaging as applied to individual choice is not particularly new. In 2009, Purdue University started experimenting with something called Course Signals, an automated system that would, for example, warn students off signing up for a class if data like performance in previous courses, along with their demographic profile, suggested they were "high risk" for non-completion.

Course Signals is an example of Wilson's consilience and the economic style of thinking as applied to individual choice. If the algorithm can determine the most efficient path to a college degree, then this must be the "best" choice. Early reports from Purdue suggested that Course Signals was keeping more students on track toward graduation and was declared a success.

Never mind if the degree is in a subject you're interested in; the goal is simply to pass through the institution and get a degree of any kind. Course Signals was part of a great enthusiasm at the time for so-called learning analytics, working from data collected through learning management systems and other means that was going to get every student marching the "correct" path according to the averages.

Ultimately, Purdue's claims about increased retention due to Course Signals fell apart as they'd made a fundamental error of statistical analysis. Mike Caulfield, a professor and expert in human interactions with digital technology, discovered that taking one Course Signals course had a negative effect on retention while taking two Course Signals courses had a strongly positive effect on retention. Caulfield showed that this spike was likely due to lots of people who only took one Course Signals course, dropping out before they had a chance to take a second. That universe of people who took two Course Signals courses had already proven they were more likely to persist in their studies regardless of any other variables.[2]

That attempt to turn individuals into averages to spur increased graduation from college ended up being a significant distraction from the far more common cause of struggles with college costs and access to resources. The difficulties of persisting in college have much more to do with our needs as humans for security and shelter than our failure to behave like proper machines.

I share these examples to illustrate how the rationale and mindset behind algorithmic control is nothing new. The only difference with generative AI over these earlier big data experiments is in the processing power of the algorithm. But there is no amount of processing power that can wash away the risks that come with reducing individuals to averages.

One of the ideas we must renew is that we are not the sum total of our averages. When we reduce individuals to averages and then constrain their behaviors based on those averages, we are restricting freedoms. Generative AI content is, by definition, a great averaging of what's in the world. An embrace of this output is a kind of capitulation to the machine, rather than staying true to our nature as creatures.

An important way to reconnect with our creature selves is to plot an escape from a world where our primary source of experience and information comes via an algorithm, something known as Filterworld.

YOU GOTTA HAVE TASTE

When it comes to books, I have good taste.

Better than good. My taste is truly excellent.

This is not a humblebrag or even a straight-up brag; it's essentially a fact. I know what books I like, and I can tell you why I think the books are good. This is the core of my success as a professional recommender of books in my column at the *Chicago Tribune* and my associated newsletter, *The Biblioracle Recommends*. When someone sends me their list of five recently read books and I make a recommendation, it is not a stab in the dark. It is a combination of calculated and intuitive responses based in the fact of my excellent taste in books.

It's important to not confuse my declaration of having good taste with a claim that my taste is somehow universal. There are many books that I think are great that other people don't, and vice versa. When I talk about taste, I am not talking about infallible judgment but instead something deeply personal. I am in touch with what I like to read and why, and I can translate that self-knowledge to what I recommend others should read. My taste in books is mine.

And also, it is very good. It is good *because* it is mine. I have been allowed to shape it according to my own interests and needs, ranging freely as a reader since I was a small child and having the opportunity to explore my taste by writing about it in various contexts. Good taste, meaning your own taste, is much like writing; it is developed through experience, exploration, and practice.

In *Filterworld: How Algorithms Flattened Culture*, Kyle Chayka, a staff writer for the *New Yorker*, charts the rise of "algorithmic recommendations" and how recommendation engines now dominate in terms of the media and content we are exposed to on a daily (or really, minute-by-minute) basis. Our social media feeds are governed by opaque (and often changeable) algorithms. The music Spotify feeds us and the shows Netflix brings to our attention are driven by algorithms. If you open a book on a Kindle, you are prodded to see what passages other people have highlighted most often. The message is clear: everyone else thinks this stuff is good.

Chayka calls our algorithm-mediated experiences in life Filterworld, and the effects go even beyond digital spaces, such as what Chayka calls the Generic Coffee Shop:

> White subway tiles lining the walls, broad industrial tables made of reclaimed wood, mid-century modern chairs with spindly legs, and hanging pendant lamps fitted with Edison bulbs.[3]

Chayka encountered this "Instagrammy aesthetic" during reporting travels across the globe—"Kyoto, Berlin, Beijing, Reykjavik, Los Angeles"—and once inside saw a lot of people who looked like he did, "freelancers tapping at their laptops, often surfing social media."

Chayka says, "The culture of Filterworld is the culture of presets, established patterns that get repeated again and again. The technology limits us to certain modes of consumption; you can't stray outside the lines." Straying outside the lines can result in "algorithmic anxiety" as we sense we're deviating from some kind of established norm, rather than simply expressing a personal preference.

The first step to moving beyond Filterworld is to start to recognize when and how we are being steered by the algorithms. The next step is to do the work of identifying and understanding and owning your own taste.

Here are two statements regarding taste that some will find contradictory:

1. I have good taste in music.
2. I like the jam band Phish.

Telling someone who is super into music that you like Phish is like telling someone super into cooking that you like to eat rotten entrails. In some corners, liking Phish is disqualifying when it comes to being able to say you have *good taste* in music.

But it's important to recognize that the goal of developing one's own taste is not to ultimately land on what other people think is good. Your taste belongs to you. I like listening to Phish. I dig the jams. I could cite how every year they play four consecutive nights of sold-out shows at Madison Square Garden over New Year's Eve to show that I'm not alone, but who cares? It's enough if you know why you like something and, perhaps more importantly, to not let some kind of outside consensus steer you away from your own taste.

This process may literally be foreign to someone who has grown up almost entirely in Filterworld. This sometimes results in discussions around content that get mired in unproductive tugs-of-war about ideology rather than exploratory journeys deep into aesthetics that invoke deeper, more lasting values and provide individuals a place from which to process the world and their place in it.

If we are going to organize a response in education around things generative AI can't do—and will never be able to do—perhaps we should focus on helping students develop their tastes.

In my observation, many young people have been denied access to their tastes inside school writing contexts. This is sort of tragic, given that shaping and expressing one's taste requires the kind of deep critical thinking we say we want students to develop.

For example, I started all my creative writing classes with a little preamble on art mostly cribbed (with attribution) from that Tolstoy treatise *What Is Art?* in which I would say something along the lines of "Art is to be experienced, but not necessarily understood," and I was often struck by how odd that sounded to students inside a classroom context. They'd only been asked to explain what a text meant, and the idea that they could have a personal experience with a text seemed strange.

Developing taste requires practice. Once you encounter a new work, you need to be willing to trust your own reaction and then to explore that reaction. Over time, that process will reveal your taste to you, and with enough practice, you will become increasingly attuned to it. The react, observe, analyze, synthesize sequence discussed earlier is a good way to consider your own taste. When you react, what are you reacting to? What part of your creature self is being stimulated by the thing you are reading? In many cases, we have a well-developed taste that we just haven't taken the time to consider. This consideration can help us get in better touch with what kind of writing we gravitate toward and make it easier to find and connect to this writing.

This is not easy work in today's world. Avoiding the influence of the algorithm requires a conscious effort of resistance. Getting a book recommendation from your local bookseller or librarian or friend is a small act of resisting the algorithm.

The danger of introducing something like AI feedback on student writing is to create a kind of "official" definition of taste as determined by the algorithm. If the imperative of school is to please the algorithm, we will have generations of students who have never even had a chance to explore their own tastes through attempts at expression. It is bad that school is already largely like this. Enshrining this antihuman attitude in a teaching machine would be beyond disastrous.

I feel fortunate that I had many years of exploring my own tastes prior to the rise of social media and algorithm-mediated content. One of the things we will need to renew to make these algorithm-free experiences possible is a sense of community.

SHRINKING THE CIRCLE

When I was growing up in the 1970s and 1980s, when it came to finding new music, I had no algorithm, but I did have a four-years-older brother, which was much better.

Better from my perspective anyway, though I'm not sure how thrilled my parents were about us blasting AC/DC and Queen and then Prince, U2, and the Replacements from my brother's stereo. Later, when listening to music together became a pastime for my friends and me, we would immerse ourselves in the work of Jimi Hendrix, the Beatles, and also R.E.M.

When one of us heard something new, we would bring it to the group for discussion and dissection. Listening to Jimi Hendrix led us to Stevie Ray Vaughan, who was the first concert I ever went to once I could drive. There was not always strong group consensus on who was good and who was bad. I had a secret love for Phil Collins and Tears for Fears that I did not share with the group. Later in college, my friend Steve told me about this band from Vermont that was kind of cool, Phish. The rest of our friends hate Phish to this day.

Renewing our sense of community independent of the looming presence of the algorithm is a way to give ourselves some ground to stand on as we evaluate the usefulness of the technology to the experiences of our lives.

Cal Newport, a computer science professor from Georgetown University and author of a series of books designed to help people manage the overload of digital information (including *Digital Minimalism: Choosing a Focused Life in a Noisy World*), thinks we may have turned a corner and entered a new era of how we seek out and engage with information:

> Between 2012 to 2022, we came to believe that the natural structure for online interaction was for billions of people to all use the same small number of privately-owned social platforms. We're increasingly realizing now that it was this centralization idea itself that was unnatural. The underlying architecture of the internet already provides a universal platform on which anyone can talk to anyone else about any topic. We didn't additionally need all of these conversations to be consolidated into the same interfaces and curated by the same algorithms.[4]

Newport sees a future of mini-communities where audiences cluster, perhaps around an author or shared passion for subject matter that becomes not an adjunct to mass media as they are currently but a new and different media ecosystem, or more accurately, a return to earlier eras long prior to the rise of mass media. This may look more like the early internet of individuals making bespoke websites or doing their writing on blogs for attention only.

Regardless of what form it takes, there must be some value proposition for what we do, what we consume, what we like (and love) beyond the aggregations of an algorithm.

TASTE, SPECIALIZATION, EXPERIENCE

Choosing to forgo the algorithm and to *not* find value in the great averaging that's embodied in generative AI would require us to acknowledge and embrace that there are some things we won't know and that we don't need to know. For Wendell Berry, this is only natural, even desirable:

> You can't think, read, research, study, learn, or teach everything. To choose one thing is to choose against many things. To know some things well is to know other things not so well, or not at all. Knowledge is always surrounded by ignorance.[5]

Champions of artificial intelligence will tout the ability to give ourselves access to all the world's knowledge, assuming this is an unalloyed good, but what are we as individuals supposed to do with this bounty?

It's interesting to think about this kind of "ignorance," one born of choice rooted in affinity or interest with what Berry argues is a different brand of ignorance, a thoughtlessness attached to the view that technological change is "inevitable."

> That use of the word "inevitable" obviates the need to consider any alternative, and a person confronting only a single possibility is well beyond any need to think. The message is: "The machine is coming. If you are small, and in the way, you must lie down and be run over." So high a level of mental activity is readily achieved by terrapins.[6]

I was struck by the marketing copy for Khanmigo founder Sal Khan's book *Brave New Words: How AI Will Revolutionize Education (and Why That's a Good Thing)* that starts with "Whether we like it or not, the AI revolution is coming to education."

Whether we like it or not. Khan apparently sees us as so many turtles, lined up, ready to be squashed.

The book tells us why we should "embrace" and "adapt" to AI as though we are now subject to its alien presence rather than remaining in charge of our own destinies and desires. This framing suggests that our explorations are over now that AI has arrived, but I believe the opposite and that our explorations have just barely begun.

Khan's inevitability is a kind of surrender of our individual selves, as we are now to be judged by our experiences inside his educational algorithm. We will be stamped as certified, but what relationship does this have to living a good life?

In my view, the goal is to create ourselves as individuals through acts of personal discernment. To practice our taste and express our values. We bring these individual selves into communities of other individuals who have their own unique worldviews. Here, then, is an ecosystem of interdependent individuals, a collection of intelligences existing without being flattened into an algorithm.

CHAPTER 20

Explore

If I'm being honest, at times, I would wish for the power to make generative AI disappear. I suppose I am skeptical enough of the claims of its boosters to still believe on balance it offers more problems than promise, when it comes to my particular interests of writing and reading. However, while the imposition of generative AI technology on our lives should not be viewed as inevitable, its existence and availability suggest that we have some duty, both collectively and individually, to explore its potential and its pitfalls.

In a conversation on Derek Thompson's *Plain English* podcast between Thompson and *New York Times* tech writer Kevin Roose, they described working with generative AI as the equivalent to having "a thousand interns." Of this state, Roose remarked, "A thousand interns can be very helpful, but it can also be quite chaotic and you could spend more time trying to manage and delegate tasks to the interns than they actually save you. . . . You have to be thoughtful about it and give it work that is very carefully scoped and defined."[1]

That episode of *Plain English* aired in November 2023, and prior to hearing Roose's analogy and the longer discussion about how these two journalists had incorporated the technology as a tool into their work, I shifted my experimenting with ChatGPT from primarily doing activities meant to explore the boundaries of the model to actively trying to find ways to integrate it into my work.

I found a number of uses for it, some of which I described in my chapter on reading. Increasingly, because of the degraded nature of Google search, I turn to it as a first resort for internet searching where I have a strong sense of what I'm looking for. Using the upgraded ChatGPT-4 model means that I can get at least some useful information to then explore further in order to guard against the ever-present threat of hallucination.

While my individual experiments prove illuminating and interesting to me, if we are truly going to get a handle on this stuff, the exploration is going to have to be a collective effort.

EMBRACE GENERATIVE AI AS A PUBLIC ISSUE

If artificial intelligence is as transformative as its proponents believe, we should be viewing its development and use not through the lens of individual adoption but as a matter of public importance.

Think of artificial intelligence as a new form of public infrastructure that requires broad discussion and regulation to ensure safe and equal access to whatever it has to offer. Obviously, this means legislative bodies at both the state and federal level should be taking up the issue, but it is also a matter of recognizing the importance of acting through the lens of a shared public problem in spaces closer to home.

I've already discussed the labor implications and the need for collective action around generative AI, but let's look more specifically at the issue of generative AI in schools. Mike Ananny, a professor of communication at USC who studies the way distribution of information shapes public attitudes and democratic outcomes, argues that we should see generative AI in schools as a "public problem."

Our discussions have to go beyond what generative AI does and how it works. We are not looking at a technical problem with a technical solution. According to Ananny,

> Public problems are collectively debated, accounted for, and managed; they are not the purview of private companies or self-identified caretakers who work on their own timelines with proprietary knowledge. Truly public problems are never outsourced to private interests or charismatic authorities.[2]

Treating generative AI as a public problem does not mean the problem is going to be more easily solved. We collectively went through a very public problem quite recently with the COVID-19 pandemic. There were many stirring moments of collective solidarity during the crisis, including direct government assistance of a kind not seen since the Great Depression, as well as the rallying of the scientific community around the need to develop a vaccine through Operation Warp Speed. These public-spirited activities significantly shortened the disruption of the pandemic, while mitigating at least some measure of the suffering, even as we must acknowledge that those mitigations were not evenly distributed and some populations were significantly more harmed than others.

We shouldn't confuse treating a public problem as a quest to find unity of opinion. This was certainly not the case with the pandemic, nor would we ever expect it to be the case in a country as vast and varied as the United States, let alone the entirety of the world. There is no end point in these discussions. And indeed, we're still arguing about the pandemic, even as the acute phase of the crisis ended years ago.

But I would argue that these contentious debates regarding the pandemic period that in many ways are still going on reflect a kind of success regarding broad public interest and investment in an event that impacted all our lives. You cannot avoid some measure of mess and even nonsense when issues are treated as public problems, but this is superior to the alternative of passively allowing those "private interests and charismatic authorities" to have their way without informed debate and the ultimate consent of the public.

If generative AI reaches the scale that its developers claim for it, it will be as impactful as any technological innovation since the commercial internet and possibly even including it. We've seen this movie before, and it didn't turn out well.

We now have many object examples of allowing technology to be developed and take hold independent of public discussion and input leading to bad, even disastrous outcomes. Consider Facebook, once hailed by founder Mark Zuckerberg as a gateway to bettering humanity by "connecting everyone." Over time, as it penetrated more and more deeply into our culture, it became the equivalent of a "nation-state,"[3] with Zuckerberg declaring that "in a lot of ways, Facebook is more like a government than a traditional company." He was not wrong. The speed with which Facebook disseminates information—often in the form of hate and misinformation—makes it an actual threat to democracy.

Consider the implications of Zuckerberg's admission. An entity with the power of a nation-state with the ability to affect the governance of countries around the world was allowed to rise up almost entirely free of government regulation or public discussion. A similar pattern repeated for generative AI could be far worse. It is a pattern already being followed, particularly in schools as all kinds of automation "solutions" are invading the teaching/learning dynamic.

A March 2024 policy brief published by the National Education Policy Center puts it plainly:

> The weight of the available evidence suggests that the current wholesale adoption of unregulated AI applications in schools poses a grave danger to democratic civil society and to individual freedom and liberty.[4]

The imposition of AI on our lives without the corresponding power to choose or regulate its presence would lead to predictably bad results.

When we have that public conversation, all voices matter, but we also have to figure out how to explore the issues in a way that allows us to use our voices purposefully and knowledgeably. To do that, we need to find our guides.

FIND YOUR GUIDES

The speed and pace with which the technology seems to be evolving, combined with all the different domains in which generative AI has applicability, makes it virtually impossible to stay on top of all the implications of the technology across all these domains.

Early on, because of my background in writing about how we teach writing, I was approached as a kind of "expert" on some of the implications for generative AI on the writing students do in school. I *was* an expert on that stuff and still am, and I deploy my expertise in many different contexts to try to help people work through those questions. I have my lane and try to do the best I can within it. This book is an example of those efforts.

But what I am not expert in is the dozens of different generative AI–enabled writing applications and programs that have sprung up in the wake of the release of ChatGPT. There are bespoke apps for research, for summarizing, for creative writing, for outlining, for brainstorming, for commenting on writing, and more. Additional applications are constantly appearing.

Knowing the limits of my expertise, and having only so much time to maintain my own expertise, I have outsourced the keeping track of these developments to others, though the people I have outsourced it to usually don't know this.

For example, when it comes to knowing what's new in terms of specific generative AI applications that relate to teaching writing, I turn to Marc Watkins, a longtime writing teacher and director of the Mississippi AI Institute. In Marc's newsletter, *Rhetorica*, he stays on top of new programs and evolutions in the technology and how it relates to the work of teaching and learning. I trust Marc because of his background in teaching writing and how I can tell from his own writing that he and I share the same underlying values around student agency and writing as thinking.

But even as we share many values, we occupy different lanes of expertise and commentary. My focus is on preserving elements of writing and reading that I believe are most meaningful whether AI exists or not and that I believe are only more essential now that AI is here. Marc's focus is on guiding us to thoughtful integration of generative AI technology into our schools and workplaces in a way that preserves the essential values of humanity and makes sure all students have access to the experiences and resources that will allow them to thrive.

I rely on Marc's guidance regarding developments I don't have time to sort out for myself.

It is important not to mistake a guide for an all-knowing sage. While it is tempting to wholly outsource the difficult work of continuously re-forming our own worldviews, letting weirdos like Joe Rogan or Jordan Peterson, or even non-weirdos like Brené Brown, substitute for your own judgment weighed against your values is a recipe for confusion and disappointment.

While I trust Marc Watkins as a person of integrity and value his perspective on these issues, this does not mean I always agree with him. He is more open to the use of generative AI in a student's developing writing process than I am, believing that because students will encounter this technology in the world, we are obligated to guide them in using it through structured instruction in school contexts. I see his point, but I am less certain about this proposition. I am of the view that building one's writing practice certainly can and perhaps should precede the imposition of this technology on the writing process.

I look at the people who seem to be using generative AI most productively now and can't help but notice that when they were developing their professional practices, none of these people were making use of generative AI, because generative AI did not exist. Derek Thompson and Kevin Roose spent years not using generative AI, and because of it, they can successfully wrangle those thousand digital interns.

My concern is that introducing generative AI too soon runs the risk of turning students as writers into the kind of "chef" I was when my wife and I were trying the HelloFresh service, writing technicians following an encoded recipe without ever learning how to cook.

That said, it's entirely possible that students will be better off the sooner we get them exploring generative AI and understanding its limits and making the choice of how to use it for themselves. This idea makes me uneasy, but I cannot say it's definitely wrong.

These are the kinds of debates we should be having as publicly as possible as often as possible. They are presently happening in many pockets of the culture, but they should be a regular part of broad public discussions, the same way it seems like everyone has a stance on an issue like whether or not smartphones should be banned in schools. When it comes to schooling, there's little doubt that generative AI will have a more significant effect than the presence of smartphones. Why shouldn't we be having this even more important discussion?

There are dozens of other guides I turn to on a practically daily basis to keep on top of the subject as I continue to share my expertise. You'll find many of them cited in this book. Others I haven't specifically mentioned include Paris Marx, a tech critic and host of the *Tech Won't Save Us* podcast who turns a skeptical eye at outsize claims of innovation and technological transformation. Marx, a longtime observer of the tech industry, is even *more* skeptical than I am and believes we are looking at an AI bubble.

Other guides include:

- Dr. Sasha Luccioni, an AI researcher working on tracking the immediate impacts of AI so we can have better public conversations based in tangible, verifiable information.
- Dr. Alex Hanna, who is focused on investigating the inherent biases that are encoded in, but also hidden from, users of generative AI applications.
- Dr. Timnit Gebru and Dr. Margaret Mitchell, who were once coheads of Google's internal AI ethics team and since being forced out of Google for coauthoring a famous paper critical of generative AI have continued their work independently.

The quest to find one's guides connects with Kyle Chayka's belief that we benefit from developing our own senses of taste independent of the algorithms that flatten the discussion and available information. In *Filterworld*, Chayka recommends cultivating an individual practice of following threads suggested by the things you are compelled by. We should be actively looking for rabbit holes to fall into and then go exploring. For example, if you like a particular musician, read interviews with them and see who *they* cite as their favorites or their influences, and then go check that out for yourself.

All these guides I've found for myself by following threads. I first encountered Emily Bender, whom I cite several times in the book, on an episode of Paris Marx's podcast. This turned me on to Bender's podcast, where I then encountered the work of Alex Hanna. You could trace just about any source in this book to another through no more than a few degrees of separation.

Pulling on these threads independent of outside recommendations and following your own interests allows for the shaping of your taste, a process that puts you in touch with your values.

It is important also to not confine your guides to those with whom you mostly agree. Ethan Mollick, a professor at Wharton Business School and author of *Co-Intelligence: Living and Working with AI*, is someone whose views regarding the potential and use of AI I fundamentally disagree with most of the time. He is a strong believer in the ability of AI to lift performance and consistently conducts and highlights research that supports this view.

Unlike Mollick, I am not impressed when a new version of generative AI scores well on benchmark tests like the SAT or even more sophisticated measurements geared to understanding AI model performance. These things have no salience to what I believe is important. They are measurements for machines, not creatures.

But it is undeniable that Mollick is a serious researcher engaged in a good-faith effort to understand the technology and what it's capable of. I am almost more obligated to read him *because* I disagree with him. I learn as much or more from his work than just about any of my other guides, even though, or perhaps precisely because, his stances put my teeth on edge.

Our communities inevitably must contain both those with whom we agree and those with whom we differ. As long as they are willing to see themselves as a member of the community with the well-being of the community in mind, they should be welcome.

Exploring should never end. By the time this book is available to readers, I will have other guides whose insights I use to shape my own views. This is really just part of the work of being human. ChatGPT exists as a kind of answer-generating machine based on a conglomeration of existing texts. My work is to continue to explore to find frontiers not yet in ChatGPT's training data.

Conclusion

THE JOURNEY NEVER ENDS

Because I am not a machine, because I do not have instant access to all the information in the world, I have no choice but to situate myself as part of other communities inside a shared ecosystem. I find this to be a superior way to spend my days, whiling my time on the questions that interest me, rather than outsourcing my mind to something that cannot think, feel, reason, or have experiences. I am more than my economic outputs. Efficiency is not a governing principle for a happy life.

I am comfortable with all the ways I will remain ignorant.

However, the fact that I am an individual embedded in a community is often fraught and frustrating. Occasionally convinced of my own correctness on issues like how we should be teaching writing, I will sometimes fantasize about having the power to impose my approach on all schools and students, everywhere. I firmly believe this would be a significant improvement on the status quo.

But it would also be an utter betrayal of the spirit that animates that which is most meaningful about the values I bring to teaching, that we are unique intelligences in the world and we should honor those unique intelligences by giving them a chance to be heard and understood as part of a larger community.

I said at the outset of this book that generative AI is an opportunity, not a threat. It is an opportunity for us to understand ourselves as humans who form communities in class, at work, online, through reading and writing. In my view, we have been largely alienated from these experiences, but that doesn't mean they are irretrievably lost.

Sometimes I think the dividing line between those who are most enthusiastic about generative AI versus those of us who are more skeptical is between those who see life as an individual quest for glory versus people like Wendell Berry who prefer the lens of community and interdependence.

On an individual quest, there is an inevitable finish line, a dragon to be slain, a ring to be hurled into a volcano, a He Who Shall Not Be Named to be vanquished. There is a great satisfaction to the conclusion of a quest narrative, evil dispatched, worlds righted, and all that. I love them as much as the next person. But I think it is a mistake to view our lives as a quest, because there is no ultimate finish line.

Well, there is *one* finish line for all of us.

The first day of my writing classes, to prepare students for the nature of the challenge in front of them, I would share a quote from Jeff O'Neal, himself a teacher of writing, that says: "You are going to spend your whole life learning how to write . . . and then you are going to die."

I wanted students well acquainted with my sense of humor at the start of our journey together, but my pedagogical aim was for students to internalize the fact that there is no terminal proficiency when it comes to writing, that in fact proficiency isn't a goal at all. The goal is to stay invested and involved in the process, bringing us back to Thomas Mann's aphorism, "A writer is a person for whom writing is more difficult than it is for other people."

I can testify that writing involves a wonderful kind of difficulty in which our grasp continuously falls short of our reach. I am mere moments from wrapping up the bulk of my work on this book save the inevitable fine-tuning of the editorial process, and because writing is thinking and feeling as part of an embodied process, I am experiencing a kind of buzzing sensation in my head and my hands as my body senses the end of a long, intense process.

What a privilege it has been to put every ounce of myself into the effort.

I am hoping the book is suffused with sufficient power and wisdom to move readers to act, that I will have achieved these things with my words from my brain reflecting my understanding of the world.

It is really quite exciting to feel this potential in something I've done. It is almost like I've completed a quest.

But this is merely the end to a book, not the completion of a quest. I wish I could say there is a finish line to this work, but it is an ongoing process. We never get to stop exploring, nor should we wish to.

Our individual ends are assured, but along the way to that inevitability, we should at the very least give ourselves the best chance possible to *live.*

ACKNOWLEDGMENTS

A book really takes a village, and these are just some of this village's inhabitants.

Many thanks and gratitude to:

Doug Lederman and Scott Jaschik, cofounders of Inside Higher Ed, who first gave me a regular public outlet to do my thinking about issues of importance.

Mel Flashman, for recognizing the potential of the book and shepherding it to the right publisher.

Marc Watkins, Danny Anderson, and Andrew Duval, for early reads of the original manuscript.

My editor, Emily Bender, and the entire crew at Basic Books, for their energy, their care, and their support of books that try to say something meaningful to the world.

Everyone whose work is cited in this book. The ideas of other unique intelligences are necessary for shaping ideas of my own.

And of course, thanks to Kathy, whose support makes doing something foolish like writing a book possible.

NOTES

Introduction

1. Herman, Daniel. "The End of High-School English." *Atlantic*, December 9, 2022. https://www.theatlantic.com/technology/archive/2022/12/openai-chatgpt-writing-high-school-english-essay/672412/.

2. Marche, Stephen. "The College Essay Is Dead." *Atlantic*, December 6, 2022. https://www.theatlantic.com/technology/archive/2022/12/chatgpt-ai-writing-college-student-essays/672371/.

3. Khan, Sal. "How AI Could Save (Not Destroy) Education." Filmed April 2023. TED video, 15:51. https://www.ted.com/talks/sal_khan_how_ai_could_save_not_destroy_education.

4. Bruell, Alexandra. "BuzzFeed to Use ChatGPT Creator OpenAI to Help Create Quizzes and Other Content." *Wall Street Journal*, January 26, 2023.

5. Williams, Henry. "I'm a Copywriter. I'm Pretty Sure Artificial Intelligence Is Going to Take My Job." *Guardian*, Opinion, January 24, 2023. https://www.theguardian.com/commentisfree/2023/jan/24/chatgpt-artificial-intelligence-jobs-economy.

6. Hui, Xiang, Oren Reshef, and Luofeng Zhou. "The Short-Term Effects of Generative Artificial Intelligence on Employment: Evidence

from an Online Labor Market." SSRN scholarly paper. July 31, 2023. https://doi.org/10.2139/ssrn.4527336.

7. Weiser, Benjamin. "Here's What Happens When Your Lawyer Uses ChatGPT." *New York Times*, May 27, 2023. https://www.nytimes.com/2023/05/27/nyregion/avianca-airline-lawsuit-chatgpt.html.

8. Wells, Kate. "Eating Disorder Helpline Takes Down Chatbot After It Gave Weight Loss Advice." NPR, June 8, 2023. https://www.npr.org/2023/06/08/1181131532/eating-disorder-helpline-takes-down-chatbot-after-it-gave-weight-loss-advice.

9. Cave, Nick. "I Asked ChatGPT to Write a Song in the Style of Nick Cave and This Is What It Produced. What Do You Think?" *Red Hand Files* (blog), January 2023. https://www.theredhandfiles.com/chat-gpt-what-do-you-think/.

10. Didion, Joan. "Joan Didion: Why I Write." *Literary Hub* (blog), January 26, 2021. https://lithub.com/joan-didion-why-i-write/.

Chapter 1: Automation, Not Intelligence

1. Menand, Louis. "Is A.I. the Death of I.P.?" *New Yorker*, January 15, 2024. https://www.newyorker.com/magazine/2024/01/22/who-owns-this-sentence-a-history-of-copyrights-and-wrongs-david-bellos-alexandre-montagu-book-review.

2. Roose, Kevin. "Bing's A.I. Chat: 'I Want to Be Alive.'" *New York Times*, February 16, 2023. https://www.nytimes.com/2023/02/16/technology/bing-chatbot-transcript.html.

3. Bjarnason, Baldur. "The LLMentalist Effect: How Chat-Based Large Language Models Replicate the Mechanisms of a Psychic's Con." Out of the Software Crisis, July 4, 2023. https://softwarecrisis.dev/letters/llmentalist/.

4. Heaven, Will Douglas. "Geoffrey Hinton Tells Us Why He's Now Scared of the Tech He Helped Build." *MIT Technology Review*, May 2, 2023. Accessed March 18, 2024. https://www.technologyreview.com/2023/05/02/1072528/geoffrey-hinton-google-why-scared-ai/.

5. Wolfram, Stephen. "What Is ChatGPT Doing . . . and Why Does

It Work?" *Stephen Wolfram: Writings* (blog), February 14, 2023. https://writings.stephenwolfram.com/2023/02/what-is-chatgpt-doing-and-why-does-it-work/.

6. Bender, Emily M. "Opening Remarks on 'AI in the Workplace: New Crisis or Longstanding Challenge.'" Medium, October 6, 2023. https://medium.com/@emilymenonbender/opening-remarks-on-ai-in-the-workplace-new-crisis-or-longstanding-challenge-eb81d1bee9f.

Chapter 2: Stop, Now, Before It's Too Late!

1. Andreessen, Marc. "Why AI Will Save the World." Andreessen Horowitz, June 6, 2023. https://a16z.com/ai-will-save-the-world/.

2. Roose, Kevin. "This A.I. Subculture's Motto: Go, Go, Go." *New York Times*, Technology, December 10, 2023. https://www.nytimes.com/2023/12/10/technology/ai-acceleration.html.

3. Schiff, Spencer. X post, March 16, 2024. Post deleted.

4. Vincent, James. "The Lawsuit That Could Rewrite the Rules of AI Copyright." Verge, November 8, 2022. https://www.theverge.com/2022/11/8/23446821/microsoft-openai-github-copilot-class-action-lawsuit-ai-copyright-violation-training-data.

5. Walsh, Dylan. "The Legal Issues Presented by Generative AI." *Ideas Made to Matter* (blog), March 13, 2024. https://mitsloan.mit.edu/ideas-made-to-matter/legal-issues-presented-generative-ai.

6. The New York Times v. Microsoft et al. (S.D. NY 2023). https://nytco-assets.nytimes.com/2023/12/NYT_Complaint_Dec2023.pdf.

7. "Comment from Andreessen Horowitz (a16z)." Regulations.gov. Accessed March 18, 2024. https://www.regulations.gov/comment/COLC-2023-0006-9057.

8. Kantrowitz, Alex. "The Horrific Content a Kenyan Worker Had to See While Training ChatGPT." Slate, May 21, 2023. https://slate.com/technology/2023/05/openai-chatgpt-training-kenya-traumatic.html.

9. Dzieza, Josh. "Inside the AI Factory." Verge, June 20, 2023. https://www.theverge.com/features/23764584/ai-artificial-intelligence-data-notation-labor-scale-surge-remotasks-openai-chatbots.

10. "2022 Environmental Sustainability Report." Microsoft. https://query.prod.cms.rt.microsoft.com/cms/api/am/binary/RW15mgm.

11. O'Brien, Matt, and Hannah Fingerhut. "A.I. Tools Fueled a 34% Spike in Microsoft's Water Consumption, and One City with Its Data Centers Is Concerned about the Effect on Residential Supply." *Fortune*, September 9, 2023. Accessed March 18, 2024. https://fortune.com/2023/09/09/ai-chatgpt-usage-fuels-spike-in-microsoft-water-consumption/.

12. "2023 Environmental Report—Google Sustainability." Google, July 2023. Accessed March 18, 2024. https://sustainability.google/reports/google-2023-environmental-report/.

13. O' Brien, Matt, and Hannah Fingerhut. "Artificial Intelligence Technology Behind ChatGPT Was Built in Iowa—with a Lot of Water." AP News, September 9, 2023. https://apnews.com/article/chatgpt-gpt4-iowa-ai-water-consumption-microsoft-f551fde98083d17a7e8d904f8be822c4.

14. Rojanasakul, Mira, Christopher Flavelle, Blacki Migliozzi, and Eli Murray. "America Is Using Up Its Groundwater Like There's No Tomorrow." *New York Times*, August 28, 2023. https://www.nytimes.com/interactive/2023/08/28/climate/groundwater-drying-climate-change.html.

15. Kishan, Saijel, and Josh Saul. "AI Needs So Much Power That Old Coal Plants Are Sticking Around." Bloomberg, January 25, 2024. https://www.bloomberg.com/news/articles/2024-01-25/ai-needs-so-much-power-that-old-coal-plants-are-sticking-around.

16. Tangermann, Victor. "Sam Altman Says AI Using Too Much Energy, Will Require Breakthrough Energy Source." Futurism. January 17, 2024. Accessed March 18, 2024. https://futurism.com/sam-altman-energy-breakthrough.

17. Ball, Philip. "What Is the Future of Fusion Energy?" *Scientific American*, June 1, 2023. https://www.scientificamerican.com/article/what-is-the-future-of-fusion-energy/.

18. Calma, Justine. "Microsoft Is Going Nuclear to Power Its AI Ambitions." Verge, September 26, 2023. https://www.theverge.com/2023

/9/26/23889956/microsoft-next-generation-nuclear-energy-smr-job-hiring.

19. Bender, Emily M., Timnit Gebru, Angelina McMillan-Major, and Shmargaret Shmitchell. "On the Dangers of Stochastic Parrots: Can Language Models Be Too Big? 🦜." *Proceedings of the 2021 ACM Conference on Fairness, Accountability, and Transparency*, March 2021, 610–23. https://doi.org/10.1145/3442188.3445922.

20. "Statement on AI Risk." Center for AI Safety. Accessed March 18, 2024. https://www.safe.ai/work/statement-on-ai-risk.

21. "What Are the Most Pressing World Problems?" 80,000 Hours. Updated May 2023. Accessed March 18, 2024. https://80000hours.org/problem-profiles/.

22. Henshall, Will. "TIME100 AI 2023: Eliezer Yudkowsky." *Time*, September 7, 2023. https://time.com/collection/time100-ai/6309037/eliezer-yudkowsky/.

23. Gans, Joshua. "AI and the Paperclip Problem." CEPR, June 10, 2018. https://cepr.org/voxeu/columns/ai-and-paperclip-problem.

24. Wong, Matteo. "AI Doomerism Is a Decoy." *Atlantic*, June 2, 2023. https://www.theatlantic.com/technology/archive/2023/06/ai-regulation-sam-altman-bill-gates/674278/.

Chapter 3: A Personal History of the Automation of Writing

1. "Common Core State Standards for English Language Arts, et al." Common Core State Standards Initiative, June 2, 2010. https://corestandards.org/wp-content/uploads/2023/09/ELA_Standards1.pdf.

2. Asherson, Suzanne Baruch. "The Benefits of Cursive Go Beyond Writing." *New York Times*, Opinion, April 30, 2013. https://www.nytimes.com/roomfordebate/2013/04/30/should-schools-require-children-to-learn-cursive/the-benefits-of-cursive-go-beyond-writing.

3. Bryant, Jimmy. "Cursive Handwriting Is a Cultural Tradition Worth Preserving." *New York Times*, Opinion, April 30, 2013. https://www.nytimes.com/roomfordebate/2013/04/30/should-schools-require

-children-to-learn-cursive/cursive-handwriting-is-a-cultural-tradition-worth-preserving.

4. Trubek, Anne. "Handwriting Just Doesn't Matter." *New York Times*, Opinion, August 20, 2016. https://www.nytimes.com/2016/08/21/opinion/handwriting-just-doesnt-matter.html.

5. Aldrick, Philip. "ChatGPT Will Be the Calculator for Writing, Top Economist Says." Bloomberg, January 18, 2023. https://www.bloomberg.com/news/articles/2023-01-18/chatgpt-will-be-the-calculator-for-writing-top-economist-says.

6. Watters, Audrey. "A Brief History of Calculators in the Classroom." Hack Education, March 12, 2015. http://hackeducation.com/2015/03/12/calculators.

7. Banks, Sarah. "A Historical Analysis of Attitudes Toward the Use of Calculators in Junior High and High School Math Classrooms in the United States Since 1975." Master's of education thesis, 2011. Cedarville University, Cedarville, OH. https://digitalcommons.cedarville.edu/cgi/viewcontent.cgi?referer=http://hackeducation.com/&httpsredir=1&article=1030&context=education_theses.

Chapter 5: Writing Is Thinking

1. Ghaffary, Shirin. "Author Rebecca Solnit Found 'Half' Her Books in a Dataset Used to Develop AI." Bloomberg, October 5, 2023. https://www.bloomberg.com/news/newsletters/2023-10-05/rebecca-solnit-found-half-her-books-in-a-dataset-used-to-develop-ai.

Chapter 6: Writing Is Feeling

1. Peabody College Office of Equity, Diversity and Inclusion. "Email: Webview: Reflecting on Gun Violence and Inclusive Environments." Vanderbilt University, February 15, 2023. https://t.e2ma.net/message/ul182h/m74zooz.

Chapter 7: Writing Is a Practice

1. Ericsson, Anders, and Robert Pool. "Malcolm Gladwell Got Us

Wrong: Our Research Was Key to the 10,000-Hour Rule, but Here's What Got Oversimplified." *Salon*, April 10, 2016. https://www.salon.com/2016/04/10/malcolm_gladwell_got_us_wrong_our_research_was_key_to_the_10000_hour_rule_but_heres_what_got_oversimplified/.

2. Macnamara, B. N., D. Z. Hambrick, and F. L. Oswald. "Deliberate Practice and Performance in Music, Games, Sports, Education, and Professions: A Meta-Analysis Psychological Science." *Psychological Science* 25, no. 8 (2014): 1608–18. https://doi.org/10.1177/0956797614535810.

3. Duckworth, Angela Lee. "Grit: The Power of Passion and Perseverance." Filmed April 2013. TED video, 5:59. https://www.ted.com/talks/angela_lee_duckworth_grit_the_power_of_passion_and_perseverance/transcript.

4. Zernike, Kate. "Testing for Joy and Grit? Schools Nationwide Push to Measure Students' Emotional Skills." *New York Times*, March 1, 2016. https://www.nytimes.com/2016/03/01/us/testing-for-joy-and-grit-schools-nationwide-push-to-measure-students-emotional-skills.html.

5. Duckworth, Angela. "Don't Grade Schools on Grit." *New York Times*, Opinion, March 26, 2016. https://www.nytimes.com/2016/03/27/opinion/sunday/dont-grade-schools-on-grit.html.

6. Grant, Adam. *Hidden Potential: The Science of Achieving Greater Things*. New York: Viking, 2023. p. 98.

7. Grant, *Hidden Potential*. p. 100.

Chapter 8: Life with a Writing Practice

1. Hagerty, James. "Leo Shapiro Advised Retailers and Spotted 'Grazing' Trend." *Wall Street Journal*, June 10, 2016. https://www.wsj.com/articles/leo-shapiro-advised-retailers-and-spotted-grazing-trend-1465579042.

Chapter 9: Reading and Writing

1. Leichter, Hilary. "Hilary Leichter on the Partnership Between Reader and Writer." *Literary Hub* (blog), October 6, 2023. https://lithub.com/hilary-leichter-on-the-partnership-between-reader-and-writer/.

2. Houston, S. M., C. Lebel, T. Katzir, F. R. Manis, E. Kan, G. R. Rodriguez, and E. R. Sowell. "Reading Skill and Structural Brain Development." *Neuroreport* 25, no. 5 (March 26, 2014): 347–52. https://doi.org/10.1097/WNR.0000000000000121.

3. "Transcript: Ezra Klein Interviews Maryanne Wolf." *New York Times*, Opinion, November 22, 2022. https://www.nytimes.com/2022/11/22/opinion/transcript-ezra-klein-interviews-maryanne-wolf.html.

4. Diamond, Jonny. "Crypto Nerd Sam Bankman-Fried, Who Just Lost $16 Billion, 'Would Never Read a Book.'" *Literary Hub* (blog), November 11, 2022. https://lithub.com/crypto-nerd-sam-bankman-fried-who-just-lost-16-billion-would-never-read-a-book/.

5. Kreizman, Maris. "Against Disruption: On the Bulletpointization of Books." *Literary Hub* (blog), February 1, 2024. https://lithub.com/against-disruption-on-the-bulletpointization-of-books/.

Chapter 10: Reading, Writing, and Robots

1. Altman, Sam. @sama. X post, February 9, 2024, 5:55 p.m. https://x.com/sama/status/1756089361609981993.

2. Goldman, Sharon. "Sam Altman Wants up to $7 Trillion for AI chips. The Natural Resources Required Would Be 'Mind Boggling.'" VentureBeat, February 9, 2024. https://venturebeat.com/ai/sam-altman-wants-up-to-7-trillion-for-ai-chips-the-natural-resources-required-would-be-mind-boggling/.

Chapter 11: Here Come the Teaching Machines (Again)

1. Khan, Sal. "How AI Could Save (Not Destroy) Education." YouTube video, 15:36. Posted by TED, May 1, 2023. Accessed March 21, 2024. https://www.youtube.com/watch?v=hJP5GqnTrNo.

2. Wan, Tony. "Knewton Was Acquired for Less than $17M, and Former CEO Brian Kibby Has Left." EdSurge, September 7, 2019.

3. Watters, Audrey. *Teaching Machines: The History of Personalized Learning*. Cambridge, MA: MIT Press, 2021. p. 150.

4. Watters. *Teaching Machines*. p. 153.

5. Watters. *Teaching Machines*. p. 45.

6. Leckart, Steven. "The Stanford Education Experiment Could Change Higher Learning Forever." *Wired*, March 20, 2012. Accessed March 21, 2024. https://www.wired.com/2012/03/ff-aiclass/.

7. Chafkin, Max. "Udacity's Sebastian Thrun, Godfather of Free Online Education, Changes Course." *Fast Company*, November 14, 2013. https://www.fastcompany.com/3021473/udacity-sebastian-thrun-uphill-climb.

8. Toppo, Greg. "A Cautionary Tale: Why IBM's Dazzling Watson Supercomputer Made a Lousy Tutor." The 74, April 9, 2024. https://www.the74million.org/article/a-cautionary-ai-tale-why-ibms-dazzling-watson-supercomputer-made-a-lousy-tutor/.

9. Hess, Rick. "A Confession and a Question on Personalized Learning." *Education Week*, February 12, 2018. https://www.edweek.org/leadership/opinion-a-confession-and-a-question-on-personalized-learning/2018/02.

10. Meyer, Dan. "The Misunderstanding About Education That Cost Mark Zuckerberg $100 Million." *Mathworlds* (blog), October 11, 2023. https://danmeyer.substack.com/p/the-misunderstanding-about-education.

Chapter 12: Writing in the Classroom of Today (and Tomorrow)

1. Clune, Michael W. "AI Means Professors Need to Raise Their Grading Standards." *Chronicle of Higher Education*, September 12, 2023. https://www.chronicle.com/article/ai-means-professors-need-to-raise-their-grading-standards.

2. Barton, Aden. "AWOL from Academics." *Harvard Magazine*, February 7, 2024. https://www.harvardmagazine.com/node/85660.

3. Hodges, Tim. "School Engagement Is More Than Just Talk." Gallup, October 25, 2018. https://www.gallup.com/education/244022/school-engagement-talk.aspx.

4. "Stress in America 2013 Highlights: Are Teens Adopting Adults' Stress Habits?" American Psychological Association. Accessed March 21, 2024. https://www.apa.org/news/press/releases/stress/2013/highlights.

5. American College Health Association. *American College Health Association—National College Health Assessment II: Reference Group Executive Summary Spring 2018*. Silver Spring, MD: American College Health Association, 2018. https://www.acha.org/documents/ncha/NCHA-II_Spring_2018_Reference_Group_Executive_Summary.pdf.

6. Black, Tyler. "Children's Risk of Suicide Increases on School Days." *Scientific American*, August 22, 2022. https://www.scientificamerican.com/article/childrens-risk-of-suicide-increases-on-school-days/.

7. Roeloffs, Mary Whitfill. "Teen Suicide Plummeted During Covid-19 School Closures, New Study Finds." *Forbes*, July 19, 2023. https://www.forbes.com/sites/maryroeloffs/2023/07/19/teen-suicide-plummeted-during-covid-19-school-closures-new-study-finds/.

8. Meyer, Dan. "Why Generative AI Will Underperform Expectations in Education." *Mathworlds* (blog), July 19, 2023. https://danmeyer.substack.com/p/why-generative-ai-will-underperform.

Chapter 13: Reading Like a Writer

1. Cohen, Rachel M. "The New 'Science of Reading' Movement, Explained." Vox, August 15, 2023. https://www.vox.com/23815311/science-of-reading-movement-literacy-learning-loss.

2. Wyse, Dominic, and Alice Bradbury. "Reading Wars or Reading Reconciliation? A Critical Examination of Robust Research Evidence, Curriculum Policy and Teachers' Practices for Teaching Phonics and Reading." *Review of Education* 10, no. 1 (April 2022): e3314. https://doi.org/10.1002/rev3.3314.

3. "NAEP Long-Term Trends: Student Experiences." Nation's Report Card. Accessed March 22, 2024. https://www.nationsreportcard.gov/ltt/reading/student-experiences/?age=9.

4. Elsen-Rooney, Michael. "Some NYC High Schools Are Shaking up Their Approach to English Class." Chalkbeat, August 8, 2023. https://www.chalkbeat.org/newyork/2023/8/8/23825097/nyc-high-school-literacy-curriculum-reading/.

5. Kotsko, Adam. "The Loss of Things I Took for Granted." Slate,

February 11, 2024. https://slate.com/human-interest/2024/02/literacy-crisis-reading-comprehension-college.html.

6. Holmes, Linda. "What Those George Clooney Jokes Know About Red Carpet Culture." NPR, January 12, 2015. https://www.npr.org/2015/01/12/376718642/what-those-george-clooney-jokes-know-about-red-carpet-culture.

7. Wallace, David Foster. *A Supposedly Fun Thing I'll Never Do Again.* Boston: Back Bay Books, 1998. p. 256.

Chapter 14: Content vs. Writing

1. Lewis, Amanda Chicago. "The People Who Ruined the Internet." Verge, November 1, 2023. https://www.theverge.com/features/23931789/seo-search-engine-optimization-experts-google-results.

2. Ward, Jake. @jakezward. X post, November 24, 2023, 7:47 A.M. https://x.com/jakezward/status/1728032634037567509?s=20.

3. Mollick, Ethan. @emollick. X post, November 26, 2023, 7:48 P.M. https://x.com/emollick/status/1728938897777045881?s=20.

4. Ortiz, Drew. "The Best Full-Size Volleyballs for 2022." *Sports Illustrated*, October 4, 2022. https://web.archive.org/web/20221004090814/https://www.si.com/review/full-size-volleyball/.

5. Dupré, Maggie Harrison. "Sports Illustrated Published Articles by Fake, AI-Generated Writers." Futurism, November 27, 2023. https://futurism.com/sports-illustrated-ai-generated-writers.

6. Sports Illustrated. @SInow. X post, November 27, 2023, 6:06 P.M. https://twitter.com/SInow/status/1729275460922622374.

7. Sato, Mia. "When a Funeral Is Clickbait." Verge, February 12, 2024. https://www.theverge.com/24065145/ai-obituary-spam-generative-clickbait.

8. Friedman, Jane. "I Would Rather See My Books Get Pirated Than This (Or: Why Goodreads and Amazon Are Becoming Dumpster Fires)." *Jane Friedman* (blog), August 7, 2023. https://janefriedman.com/i-would-rather-see-my-books-pirated/.

9. Duffy, Clare. "An Author Says AI Is 'Writing' Unauthorized Books

Being Sold under Her Name on Amazon." CNN, August 10, 2023. https://www.cnn.com/2023/08/10/tech/ai-generated-books-amazon/index.html.

Chapter 15: On the Future of Writing for Money

1. "Marine Biologist Demographics and Statistics [2024]: Number Of Marine Biologists in the US." Zippia, January 29, 2021. https://www.zippia.com/marine-biologist-jobs/demographics/.

2. Walker, Mason. "U.S. Newsroom Employment Has Fallen 26% Since 2008." Pew Research Center, July 13, 2021. Accessed March 22, 2024. https://www.pewresearch.org/short-reads/2021/07/13/u-s-newsroom-employment-has-fallen-26-since-2008/.

3. Milliot, Jim. "Writing Books Remains a Tough Way to Make a Living." *Publishers Weekly*, September 29, 2023. https://www.publishersweekly.com/pw/by-topic/industry-news/publisher-news/article/93301-author-incomes-post-small-gains.html.

4. Zacks, Richard. "The 19th-Century Start-Ups That Cost Mark Twain His Fortune." *Time*, April 19, 2016. https://time.com/4297572/mark-twain-bad-business/.

5. Sanderson, Brandon. "Surprise! Four Secret Novels by Brandon Sanderson." Kickstarter. Updated March 5, 2024. https://www.kickstarter.com/projects/dragonsteel/surprise-four-secret-novels-by-brandon-sanderson.

6. Milliot, Jim. "Self-Publishing Is Thriving, According to Bowker Report." *Publishers Weekly*, February 17, 2023. https://www.publishersweekly.com/pw/by-topic/industry-news/publisher-news/article/91574-self-publishing-is-thriving-according-to-bowker-report.html.

7. Lopatto, Elizabeth. "How Much Money Do We Think Substack Lost Last Year?" Verge, March 28, 2023. https://www.theverge.com/2023/3/28/23660473/substack-retail-investors-revenue-profit.

8. Doctorow, Cory. "The Big Lie That Keeps the Uber Bezzle Alive." Medium, February 11, 2022. https://doctorow.medium.com/the-big-lie-that-keeps-the-uber-bezzle-alive-8d6e8c0ccde7.

9. Ley, Tom. "How We Got Here." Defector, September 8, 2020. https://defector.com/how-we-got-here.

Chapter 18: Resist

1. Metz, Cade. "A.I. Start-Up Anthropic Challenges OpenAI and Google With New Chatbot." *New York Times*, March 4, 2024. https://www.nytimes.com/2024/03/04/technology/anthropic-claude-openai-google.html.

2. Warren, Tamara. "The US Secretary of Transportation on a Driverless America." Verge, November 1, 2016. http://www.theverge.com/a/verge-2021/secretary-anthony-foxx.

3. Associated Press. "Cruise Recalls All Self-Driving Cars after Grisly Accident and California Ban." *Guardian*, November 8, 2023. https://www.theguardian.com/technology/2023/nov/08/cruise-recall-self-driving-cars-gm.

4. Karpf, Dave. "The Myth of Technological Inevitability." *The Future, Now and Then* (blog), January 24, 2024. https://davekarpf.substack.com/p/the-myth-of-technological-inevitability.

5. Barnum, Matt. "This Tech Evangelist Has Big Dreams for AI Tutors. Are They Too Big?" *Wall Street Journal*, March 7, 2024. https://www.wsj.com/us-news/education/sal-khan-has-big-dreams-for-ai-in-education-are-they-too-big-41f01fb9.

6. Texas Education Agency Student Assessment Division. "Scoring Process for STAAR Constructed Responses." Texas Education Agency. December 2023. https://tea.texas.gov/student-assessment/testing/staar/scoring-process-staar-constructed-response.pdf.

7. Steiss, Jacob, Tamara Tate, Steve Graham, Jazmin Cruz, Michael Hebert, Jiali Wang, Youngsun Moon, Waverly Tseng, Mark Warschauer, and Carol Booth Olson. "Comparing the Quality of Human and ChatGPT Feedback of Students' Writing." *Learning and Instruction* 91 (June 1, 2024): 101894. https://doi.org/10.1016/j.learninstruc.2024.101894.

Chapter 19: Renew

1. Berry, Wendell. *Life Is a Miracle: An Essay Against Modern Superstition*. Washington, DC: Counterpoint, 2001. p. 48.

2. Caulfield, Michael. "Why the Course Signals Math Does Not Add Up." *Hapgood* (blog), September 26, 2013. https://hapgood.us/2013/09/26/why-the-course-signals-math-does-not-add-up/.

3. Chayka, Kyle. *Filterworld: How Algorithms Flattened Culture*. New York: Doubleday, 2024. p. 5.

4. Newport, Cal. "Neil Gaiman's Radical Vision for the Future of the Internet." *Cal Newport* (blog), November 27, 2023. https://calnewport.com/neil-gaimans-radical-vision-for-the-future-of-the-internet/.

5. Berry. *Life Is a Miracle*. p. 60.

6. Berry. *Life Is a Miracle*. p. 53.

Chapter 20: Explore

1. Thompson, Derek. "How ChatGPT Can Change the Future of Jobs—Starting with Your Own." Ringer, November 14, 2023. https://www.theringer.com/2023/11/14/23959761/chatgpt-future-of-jobs-ai-tools.

2. Schoenberg, Kelsey. "To Reckon with Generative AI, Make It a Public Problem." *Issues in Science and Technology*, January 16, 2024. https://issues.org/ai-public-problem-ananny/.

3. Farrell, Henry, Margaret Levi, and Tim O'Reilly. "Mark Zuckerberg Runs a Nation-State, and He's the King." Vox, April 9, 2018. https://www.vox.com/the-big-idea/2018/4/9/17214752/zuckerberg-facebook-power-regulation-data-privacy-control-political-theory-data-breach-king.

4. Williamson, Ben, Alex Molnar, and Faith Boninger. "Time for a Pause: Without Effective Public Oversight, AI in Schools Will Do More Harm Than Good." National Education Policy Cetner, March 5, 2024. https://nepc.colorado.edu/publication/ai.

INDEX

John Warner is a writer, speaker, researcher, and consultant. The former editor of *McSweeney's Internet Tendency*, he is the author of the books *Why They Can't Write* and *The Writer's Practice*. As "the Biblioracle," Warner is a weekly columnist at the *Chicago Tribune* and writes the newsletter *The Biblioracle Recommends*. He is affiliate faculty at the College of Charleston and lives in Folly Beach, South Carolina.